# TREASURED
## *Psalms*
## *&*
## *Proverbs*

# TREASURED

## Psalms
### &
## Proverbs

BARBOUR
PUBLISHING

© 2011 by Barbour Publishing, Inc.

ISBN 978-1-61626-208-2

All scripture quotations are taken from the King James Version of the Bible.

Published by Barbour Publishing, Inc., P.O. Box 719, Uhrichsville, Ohio 44683 www.barbourbooks.com

*Our mission is to publish and distribute inspirational products offering exceptional value and biblical encouragement to the masses.*

Member of the
Evangelical Christian
Publishers Association

Printed in the United States of America.

# Contents

Welcome to

## TREASURED

# Psalms
# & Proverbs

When you need encouragement, enlightenment, and edification, look to this little volume—it contains the best of the best of scripture's wisdom books.

This handy resource presents some of the most uplifting and helpful portions of the Psalms and Proverbs, all in the beautiful and beloved language of the King James Version. And each passage is accompanied by a brief explanatory note that helps to put its message into a clearer context.

For nearly three millennia, God's people have found comfort and hope in the Psalms and Proverbs—and so can you. Each passage that follows is sure to give you a spiritual boost, whatever the circumstances of your day.

# PSALM 1

*Throughout scripture, God calls His people to set
their standards higher than those of the world in
general. People who commit themselves to God and
are obedient to His clear instructions are promised
rewards; those who reject Him can expect judgment.*

¹Blessed is the man that walketh not in the
counsel of the ungodly, nor standeth in the way of
sinners, nor sitteth in the seat of the scornful.
²But his delight is in the law of the LORD; and in
his law doth he meditate day and night.
³And he shall be like a tree planted by the
rivers of water, that bringeth forth his fruit in
his season; his leaf also shall not wither; and
whatsoever he doeth shall prosper.
⁴The ungodly are not so: but are like the chaff
which the wind driveth away.
⁵Therefore the ungodly shall not stand in the
judgment, nor sinners in the congregation of the
righteous.
⁶For the LORD knoweth the way of the righteous:
but the way of the ungodly shall perish.

# PSALM 3

*This is the first of seventy-three psalms designated "of David." David's confidence in God is evident in his ability to sleep at night (verses 4–6). Insomnia is one of the first side effects of worry. But rather than fretting and losing sleep, David talks to God, enabling him to find peace of mind and rest.*

¹Lord, how are they increased that trouble me! many are they that rise up against me.

²Many there be which say of my soul, There is no help for him in God. Selah.

³But thou, O Lord, art a shield for me; my glory, and the lifter up of mine head.

⁴I cried unto the Lord with my voice, and he heard me out of his holy hill. Selah.

⁵I laid me down and slept; I awaked; for the Lord sustained me.

⁶I will not be afraid of ten thousands of people, that have set themselves against me round about.

⁷Arise, O Lord; save me, O my God: for thou hast smitten all mine enemies upon the cheek bone; thou hast broken the teeth of the ungodly.

⁸Salvation belongeth unto the Lord: thy blessing is upon thy people. Selah.

*Despite the very real threat David is feeling from his enemies, in verse 17 he concludes this psalm, as psalmists so frequently do, with praise to God—and an advance acknowledgement of God's willingness to act on behalf of His faithful people.*

¹O LORD my God, in thee do I put my trust: save me from all them that persecute me, and deliver me:
²Lest he tear my soul like a lion, rending it in pieces, while there is none to deliver.
³O LORD my God, if I have done this; if there be iniquity in my hands;
⁴If I have rewarded evil unto him that was at peace with me; (yea, I have delivered him that without cause is mine enemy:)
⁵Let the enemy persecute my soul, and take it; yea, let him tread down my life upon the earth, and lay mine honour in the dust. Selah.
⁶Arise, O LORD, in thine anger, lift up thyself because of the rage of mine enemies: and awake for me to the judgment that thou hast commanded.
⁷So shall the congregation of the people compass thee about: for their sakes therefore return thou on high.
⁸The LORD shall judge the people: judge me, O LORD, according to my righteousness, and according to mine integrity that is in me.
⁹Oh let the wickedness of the wicked come to an end; but establish the just: for the righteous God

trieth the hearts and reins.

<sup>10</sup>My defence is of God, which saveth the upright in heart.

<sup>11</sup>God judgeth the righteous, and God is angry with the wicked every day.

<sup>12</sup>If he turn not, he will whet his sword; he hath bent his bow, and made it ready.

<sup>13</sup>He hath also prepared for him the instruments of death; he ordaineth his arrows against the persecutors.

<sup>14</sup>Behold, he travaileth with iniquity, and hath conceived mischief, and brought forth falsehood.

<sup>15</sup>He made a pit, and digged it, and is fallen into the ditch which he made.

<sup>16</sup>His mischief shall return upon his own head, and his violent dealing shall come down upon his own pate.

<sup>17</sup>I will praise the LORD according to his righteousness: and will sing praise to the name of the LORD most high.

# PSALM 8

*Who hasn't stared into the heavens on a clear night
and wondered about the nature of God, the origin of
humanity, and other weighty questions?
This psalm reflects David's musings about such things.
David begins with an acknowledgment
that the earth is God's. When God's presence is not
considered, people come up with distorted answers to
the question, "What is man?"*

¹O LORD, our Lord, how excellent is thy name in all the earth! who hast set thy glory above the heavens.

²Out of the mouth of babes and sucklings hast thou ordained strength because of thine enemies, that thou mightest still the enemy and the avenger.

³When I consider thy heavens, the work of thy fingers, the moon and the stars, which thou hast ordained;

⁴What is man, that thou art mindful of him? and the son of man, that thou visitest him?

⁵For thou hast made him a little lower than the angels, and hast crowned him with glory and honour.

⁶Thou madest him to have dominion over the works of thy hands; thou hast put all things under his feet:

⁷All sheep and oxen, yea, and the beasts of the field;

⁸The fowl of the air, and the fish of the sea, and whatsoever passeth through the paths of the seas.

⁹O LORD our Lord, how excellent is thy name in all the earth!

# Psalm 9

*Like several of the preceding psalms of David,
Psalm 9 also deals with his struggles to endure the
persecution of his enemies. In this case, however,
David is eager to sing and rejoice because God has
dealt with David's foes. They have not only been
defeated but also rebuked, destroyed, and blotted out.
Their ruin is endless, and soon there
would not even be a memory of them.*

¹I will praise thee, O Lord, with my whole heart;
I will shew forth all thy marvellous works.
²I will be glad and rejoice in thee: I will sing
praise to thy name, O thou most High.
³When mine enemies are turned back, they shall
fall and perish at thy presence.
⁴For thou hast maintained my right and my cause;
thou satest in the throne judging right.
⁵Thou hast rebuked the heathen, thou hast
destroyed the wicked, thou hast put out their
name for ever and ever.
⁶O thou enemy, destructions are come to a
perpetual end: and thou hast destroyed cities;
their memorial is perished with them.
⁷But the Lord shall endure for ever: he hath
prepared his throne for judgment.
⁸And he shall judge the world in righteousness,
he shall minister judgment to the people in
uprightness.
⁹The Lord also will be a refuge for the oppressed,
a refuge in times of trouble.
¹⁰And they that know thy name will put their

trust in thee: for thou, Lord, hast not forsaken them that seek thee.

¹¹Sing praises to the Lord, which dwelleth in Zion: declare among the people his doings.

¹²When he maketh inquisition for blood, he remembereth them: he forgetteth not the cry of the humble.

¹³Have mercy upon me, O Lord; consider my trouble which I suffer of them that hate me, thou that liftest me up from the gates of death:

¹⁴That I may shew forth all thy praise in the gates of the daughter of Zion: I will rejoice in thy salvation.

¹⁵The heathen are sunk down in the pit that they made: in the net which they hid is their own foot taken.

¹⁶The Lord is known by the judgment which he executeth: the wicked is snared in the work of his own hands. Higgaion. Selah.

¹⁷The wicked shall be turned into hell, and all the nations that forget God.

¹⁸For the needy shall not always be forgotten: the expectation of the poor shall not perish for ever.

¹⁹Arise, O Lord; let not man prevail: let the heathen be judged in thy sight.

²⁰Put them in fear, O Lord: that the nations may know themselves to be but men. Selah.

*The opening statement of Psalm 11 is David's theme:*
*"In the Lord put I my trust." Even though earthly*
*events may seem to be more chaotic and turbulent than*
*usual, one's spiritual condition is as reliable as ever. God*
*is still on His throne. Nothing has changed. He sees*
*what is going on, He will judge what He sees, and it*
*won't be pleasant for those who have defied Him.*

¹In the LORD put I my trust: how say ye to my
soul, Flee as a bird to your mountain?
²For, lo, the wicked bend their bow, they make
ready their arrow upon the string, that they may
privily shoot at the upright in heart.
³If the foundations be destroyed, what can the
righteous do?
⁴The LORD is in his holy temple, the LORD's
throne is in heaven: his eyes behold, his eyelids
try, the children of men.
⁵The LORD trieth the righteous: but the wicked
and him that loveth violence his soul hateth.
⁶Upon the wicked he shall rain snares, fire and
brimstone, and an horrible tempest: this shall be
the portion of their cup.
⁷For the righteous LORD loveth righteousness; his
countenance doth behold the upright.

*With so many of the previous psalms expressing the
writer's confusion, despair, and outrage over the fact
that ungodly people seem to be running rampant
while believers in God struggle to get by,
Psalm 15 is a simple but powerful reminder
of what is really important.*

¹Lord, who shall abide in thy tabernacle? who shall dwell in thy holy hill?
²He that walketh uprightly, and worketh righteousness, and speaketh the truth in his heart.
³He that backbiteth not with his tongue, nor doeth evil to his neighbour, nor taketh up a reproach against his neighbour.
⁴In whose eyes a vile person is contemned; but he honoureth them that fear the Lord. He that sweareth to his own hurt, and changeth not.
⁵He that putteth not out his money to usury, nor taketh reward against the innocent. He that doeth these things shall never be moved.

# PSALM 18

*This is another psalm about David's praise to God in gratitude for His help in dealing with aggressive enemies. David doesn't consider himself a special case to receive God's help and protection. In verses 15–27, he affirms that anyone who is faithful will witness God's faithfulness in return, and everyone who is blameless, pure, and humble stands to benefit from the righteous character of the Lord.*

¹I will love thee, O LORD, my strength.

²The LORD is my rock, and my fortress, and my deliverer; my God, my strength, in whom I will trust; my buckler, and the horn of my salvation, and my high tower.

³I will call upon the LORD, who is worthy to be praised: so shall I be saved from mine enemies.

⁴The sorrows of death compassed me, and the floods of ungodly men made me afraid.

⁵The sorrows of hell compassed me about: the snares of death prevented me.

⁶In my distress I called upon the LORD, and cried unto my God: he heard my voice out of his temple, and my cry came before him, even into his ears.

⁷Then the earth shook and trembled; the foundations also of the hills moved and were shaken, because he was wroth.

⁸There went up a smoke out of his nostrils, and fire out of his mouth devoured: coals were kindled by it.

⁹He bowed the heavens also, and came down: and darkness was under his feet.

¹⁰And he rode upon a cherub, and did fly: yea, he did fly upon the wings of the wind.

¹¹He made darkness his secret place; his pavilion round about him were dark waters and thick clouds of the skies.

¹²At the brightness that was before him his thick clouds passed, hail stones and coals of fire.

¹³The LORD also thundered in the heavens, and the Highest gave his voice; hail stones and coals of fire.

¹⁴Yea, he sent out his arrows, and scattered them; and he shot out lightnings, and discomfited them.

¹⁵Then the channels of waters were seen, and the foundations of the world were discovered at thy rebuke, O LORD, at the blast of the breath of thy nostrils.

¹⁶He sent from above, he took me, he drew me out of many waters.

¹⁷He delivered me from my strong enemy, and from them which hated me: for they were too strong for me.

¹⁸They prevented me in the day of my calamity: but the LORD was my stay.

¹⁹He brought me forth also into a large place; he delivered me, because he delighted in me.

²⁰The LORD rewarded me according to my righteousness; according to the cleanness of my hands hath he recompensed me.

²¹For I have kept the ways of the LORD, and have not wickedly departed from my God.

<sup>22</sup>For all his judgments were before me, and I did not put away his statutes from me.

<sup>23</sup>I was also upright before him, and I kept myself from mine iniquity.

<sup>24</sup>Therefore hath the LORD recompensed me according to my righteousness, according to the cleanness of my hands in his eyesight.

<sup>25</sup>With the merciful thou wilt shew thyself merciful; with an upright man thou wilt shew thyself upright;

<sup>26</sup>With the pure thou wilt shew thyself pure; and with the froward thou wilt shew thyself froward.

<sup>27</sup>For thou wilt save the afflicted people; but wilt bring down high looks.

<sup>28</sup>For thou wilt light my candle: the LORD my God will enlighten my darkness.

<sup>29</sup>For by thee I have run through a troop; and by my God have I leaped over a wall.

<sup>30</sup>As for God, his way is perfect: the word of the LORD is tried: he is a buckler to all those that trust in him.

<sup>31</sup>For who is God save the LORD? or who is a rock save our God?

<sup>32</sup>It is God that girdeth me with strength, and maketh my way perfect.

<sup>33</sup>He maketh my feet like hinds' feet, and setteth me upon my high places.

<sup>34</sup>He teacheth my hands to war, so that a bow of steel is broken by mine arms.

<sup>35</sup>Thou hast also given me the shield of thy salvation: and thy right hand hath holden me up, and thy gentleness hath made me great.

<sup>36</sup>Thou hast enlarged my steps under me, that my feet did not slip.

<sup>37</sup>I have pursued mine enemies, and overtaken them: neither did I turn again till they were consumed.

<sup>38</sup>I have wounded them that they were not able to rise: they are fallen under my feet.

<sup>39</sup>For thou hast girded me with strength unto the battle: thou hast subdued under me those that rose up against me.

<sup>40</sup>Thou hast also given me the necks of mine enemies; that I might destroy them that hate me.

<sup>41</sup>They cried, but there was none to save them: even unto the LORD, but he answered them not.

<sup>42</sup>Then did I beat them small as the dust before the wind: I did cast them out as the dirt in the streets.

<sup>43</sup>Thou hast delivered me from the strivings of the people; and thou hast made me the head of the heathen: a people whom I have not known shall serve me.

<sup>44</sup>As soon as they hear of me, they shall obey me: the strangers shall submit themselves unto me.

<sup>45</sup>The strangers shall fade away, and be afraid out of their close places.

<sup>46</sup>The LORD liveth; and blessed be my rock; and let the God of my salvation be exalted.

<sup>47</sup>It is God that avengeth me, and subdueth the people under me.

<sup>48</sup>He delivereth me from mine enemies: yea, thou liftest me up above those that rise up against me: thou hast delivered me from the violent man.

⁴⁹Therefore will I give thanks unto thee, O LORD, among the heathen, and sing praises unto thy name.
⁵⁰Great deliverance giveth he to his king; and sheweth mercy to his anointed, to David, and to his seed for evermore.

## PSALM 19

*God reveals Himself to humankind in numerous ways. In Psalm 19, David begins by giving attention to the natural world that reflects God's glory and then moves on to the revealed Word of God—the source of many various potential blessings.*

¹The heavens declare the glory of God; and the firmament sheweth his handywork.
²Day unto day uttereth speech, and night unto night sheweth knowledge.
³There is no speech nor language, where their voice is not heard.
⁴Their line is gone out through all the earth, and their words to the end of the world. In them hath he set a tabernacle for the sun,
⁵Which is as a bridegroom coming out of his chamber, and rejoiceth as a strong man to run a race.
⁶His going forth is from the end of the heaven, and his circuit unto the ends of it: and there is nothing hid from the heat thereof.

⁷The law of the Lord is perfect, converting the soul: the testimony of the Lord is sure, making wise the simple.

⁸The statutes of the Lord are right, rejoicing the heart: the commandment of the Lord is pure, enlightening the eyes.

⁹The fear of the Lord is clean, enduring for ever: the judgments of the Lord are true and righteous altogether.

¹⁰More to be desired are they than gold, yea, than much fine gold: sweeter also than honey and the honeycomb.

¹¹Moreover by them is thy servant warned: and in keeping of them there is great reward.

¹²Who can understand his errors? cleanse thou me from secret faults.

¹³Keep back thy servant also from presumptuous sins; let them not have dominion over me: then shall I be upright, and I shall be innocent from the great transgression.

¹⁴Let the words of my mouth, and the meditation of my heart, be acceptable in thy sight, O Lord, my strength, and my redeemer.

*In the opening verses of Psalm 20, it may appear that
the psalmist is offering blessings upon his readers, but
in verse 5 it becomes evident that the voice is plural,
and the message is being addressed to a singular
subject. The psalm is actually written for an assembled
group to join the king in prayer preceding a battle.*

¹The LORD hear thee in the day of trouble; the
name of the God of Jacob defend thee;
²Send thee help from the sanctuary, and
strengthen thee out of Zion;
³Remember all thy offerings, and accept thy burnt
sacrifice; Selah.
⁴Grant thee according to thine own heart, and
fulfil all thy counsel.
⁵We will rejoice in thy salvation, and in the name
of our God we will set up our banners: the LORD
fulfil all thy petitions.
⁶Now know I that the LORD saveth his anointed;
he will hear him from his holy heaven with the
saving strength of his right hand.
⁷Some trust in chariots, and some in horses: but
we will remember the name of the LORD our
God.
⁸They are brought down and fallen: but we are
risen, and stand upright.
⁹Save, LORD: let the king hear us when we call.

*Psalm 22 opens with a familiar ring, because Jesus quotes its opening line while hanging on the cross. As will soon become evident, David's words in this psalm are surprisingly descriptive of Jesus' crucifixion. Of all the psalms, this one is quoted more than any other in the New Testament.*

¹My God, my God, why hast thou forsaken me? why art thou so far from helping me, and from the words of my roaring?

²O my God, I cry in the day time, but thou hearest not; and in the night season, and am not silent.

³But thou art holy, O thou that inhabitest the praises of Israel.

⁴Our fathers trusted in thee: they trusted, and thou didst deliver them.

⁵They cried unto thee, and were delivered: they trusted in thee, and were not confounded.

⁶But I am a worm, and no man; a reproach of men, and despised of the people.

⁷All they that see me laugh me to scorn: they shoot out the lip, they shake the head, saying,

⁸He trusted on the LORD that he would deliver him: let him deliver him, seeing he delighted in him.

⁹But thou art he that took me out of the womb: thou didst make me hope when I was upon my mother's breasts.

¹⁰I was cast upon thee from the womb: thou art

my God from my mother's belly.

<sup>11</sup>Be not far from me; for trouble is near; for there is none to help.

<sup>12</sup>Many bulls have compassed me: strong bulls of Bashan have beset me round.

<sup>13</sup>They gaped upon me with their mouths, as a ravening and a roaring lion.

<sup>14</sup>I am poured out like water, and all my bones are out of joint: my heart is like wax; it is melted in the midst of my bowels.

<sup>15</sup>My strength is dried up like a potsherd; and my tongue cleaveth to my jaws; and thou hast brought me into the dust of death.

<sup>16</sup>For dogs have compassed me: the assembly of the wicked have inclosed me: they pierced my hands and my feet.

<sup>17</sup>I may tell all my bones: they look and stare upon me.

<sup>18</sup>They part my garments among them, and cast lots upon my vesture.

<sup>19</sup>But be not thou far from me, O LORD: O my strength, haste thee to help me.

<sup>20</sup>Deliver my soul from the sword; my darling from the power of the dog.

<sup>21</sup>Save me from the lion's mouth: for thou hast heard me from the horns of the unicorns.

<sup>22</sup>I will declare thy name unto my brethren: in the midst of the congregation will I praise thee.

<sup>23</sup>Ye that fear the LORD, praise him; all ye the seed of Jacob, glorify him; and fear him, all ye the seed of Israel.

<sup>24</sup>For he hath not despised nor abhorred the

affliction of the afflicted; neither hath he hid his face from him; but when he cried unto him, he heard.

²⁵My praise shall be of thee in the great congregation: I will pay my vows before them that fear him.

²⁶The meek shall eat and be satisfied: they shall praise the Lord that seek him: your heart shall live for ever.

²⁷All the ends of the world shall remember and turn unto the Lord: and all the kindreds of the nations shall worship before thee.

²⁸For the kingdom is the Lord's: and he is the governor among the nations.

²⁹All they that be fat upon earth shall eat and worship: all they that go down to the dust shall bow before him: and none can keep alive his own soul.

³⁰A seed shall serve him; it shall be accounted to the Lord for a generation.

³¹They shall come, and shall declare his righteousness unto a people that shall be born, that he hath done this.

# Psalm 23

*In what is undoubtedly the best known of the psalms,*
*David uses the imagery of a shepherd to highlight*
*God's blessings and protection of His people.*
*It was rather common for kings of the time*
*to be compared to shepherds.*
*Although King David had firsthand experience*
*in the role, in this psalm*
*he is only one of the sheep in the fold of God.*

¹The Lord is my shepherd; I shall not want.
²He maketh me to lie down in green pastures: he leadeth me beside the still waters.
³He restoreth my soul: he leadeth me in the paths of righteousness for his name's sake.
⁴Yea, though I walk through the valley of the shadow of death, I will fear no evil: for thou art with me; thy rod and thy staff they comfort me.
⁵Thou preparest a table before me in the presence of mine enemies: thou anointest my head with oil; my cup runneth over.
⁶Surely goodness and mercy shall follow me all the days of my life: and I will dwell in the house of the Lord for ever.

# Psalm 24

*Any king who approaches a city will receive
a magnificent welcome;
how much more should the nearness of
the King of glory inspire a response.
Even the gates and doors of the city are perceived as
responding to the magnitude of the event.*

¹The earth is the LORD's, and the fulness thereof;
the world, and they that dwell therein.
²For he hath founded it upon the seas, and
established it upon the floods.
³Who shall ascend into the hill of the LORD? or
who shall stand in his holy place?
⁴He that hath clean hands, and a pure heart; who
hath not lifted up his soul unto vanity, nor sworn
deceitfully.
⁵He shall receive the blessing from the LORD, and
righteousness from the God of his salvation.
⁶This is the generation of them that seek him, that
seek thy face, O Jacob. Selah.
⁷Lift up your heads, O ye gates; and be ye lift up,
ye everlasting doors; and the King of glory shall
come in.
⁸Who is this King of glory? The LORD strong and
mighty, the LORD mighty in battle.
⁹Lift up your heads, O ye gates; even lift them up,
ye everlasting doors; and the King of glory shall
come in.
¹⁰Who is this King of glory? The LORD of hosts,
he is the King of glory. Selah.

# PSALM 25

*In Psalm 25, as in many of his others, David expresses
a desire for greater closeness to God.
In the original language, the psalm is an acrostic
poem. The first verse begins with the first letter,
and following verses continue with successive letters
throughout the Hebrew alphabet.*

¹Unto thee, O LORD, do I lift up my soul.
²O my God, I trust in thee: let me not be
ashamed, let not mine enemies triumph over me.
³Yea, let none that wait on thee be ashamed: let
them be ashamed which transgress without cause.
⁴Shew me thy ways, O LORD; teach me thy paths.
⁵Lead me in thy truth, and teach me: for thou art
the God of my salvation; on thee do I wait all the
day.
⁶Remember, O LORD, thy tender mercies and thy
lovingkindnesses; for they have been ever of old.
⁷Remember not the sins of my youth, nor my
transgressions: according to thy mercy remember
thou me for thy goodness' sake, O LORD.
⁸Good and upright is the LORD: therefore will he
teach sinners in the way.
⁹The meek will he guide in judgment: and the
meek will he teach his way.
¹⁰All the paths of the LORD are mercy and
truth unto such as keep his covenant and his
testimonies.
¹¹For thy name's sake, O LORD, pardon mine

iniquity; for it is great.

¹²What man is he that feareth the Lord? him shall he teach in the way that he shall choose.

¹³His soul shall dwell at ease; and his seed shall inherit the earth.

¹⁴The secret of the Lord is with them that fear him; and he will shew them his covenant.

¹⁵Mine eyes are ever toward the Lord; for he shall pluck my feet out of the net.

¹⁶Turn thee unto me, and have mercy upon me; for I am desolate and afflicted.

¹⁷The troubles of my heart are enlarged: O bring thou me out of my distresses.

¹⁸Look upon mine affliction and my pain; and forgive all my sins.

¹⁹Consider mine enemies; for they are many; and they hate me with cruel hatred.

²⁰O keep my soul, and deliver me: let me not be ashamed; for I put my trust in thee.

²¹Let integrity and uprightness preserve me; for I wait on thee.

²²Redeem Israel, O God, out of all his troubles.

*When faced with fear, David keeps his priorities*
*straight. Verse 4 reveals his priority—a lifetime*
*relationship with God at the tabernacle.*
*His eyes aren't directed toward the approaching enemy*
*but rather toward the beauty of the Lord.*
*Consequently, he has confidence that when trouble*
*does come, God will protect and sustain him.*

¹The Lord is my light and my salvation; whom
shall I fear? the Lord is the strength of my life; of
whom shall I be afraid?
²When the wicked, even mine enemies and my
foes, came upon me to eat up my flesh, they
stumbled and fell.
³Though an host should encamp against me,
my heart shall not fear: though war should rise
against me, in this will I be confident.
⁴One thing have I desired of the Lord, that will
I seek after; that I may dwell in the house of the
Lord all the days of my life, to behold the beauty
of the Lord, and to enquire in his temple.
⁵For in the time of trouble he shall hide me in his
pavilion: in the secret of his tabernacle shall he
hide me; he shall set me up upon a rock.
⁶And now shall mine head be lifted up above
mine enemies round about me: therefore will I
offer in his tabernacle sacrifices of joy; I will sing,
yea, I will sing praises unto the Lord.
⁷Hear, O Lord, when I cry with my voice: have
mercy also upon me, and answer me.

⁸When thou saidst, Seek ye my face; my heart said unto thee, Thy face, LORD, will I seek.

⁹Hide not thy face far from me; put not thy servant away in anger: thou hast been my help; leave me not, neither forsake me, O God of my salvation.

¹⁰When my father and my mother forsake me, then the LORD will take me up.

¹¹Teach me thy way, O LORD, and lead me in a plain path, because of mine enemies.

¹²Deliver me not over unto the will of mine enemies: for false witnesses are risen up against me, and such as breathe out cruelty.

¹³I had fainted, unless I had believed to see the goodness of the LORD in the land of the living.

¹⁴Wait on the LORD: be of good courage, and he shall strengthen thine heart: wait, I say, on the LORD.

## PSALM 29

*As a pleasant end to a somewhat frightening psalm, David assures his readers in verse 11 that the all-powerful God gives strength to His people. Realizing that God is omnipotent should cause believers to rest in a consoling assurance of peace.*

¹Give unto the LORD, O ye mighty, give unto the LORD glory and strength.

²Give unto the LORD the glory due unto his name; worship the LORD in the beauty of holiness.

³The voice of the LORD is upon the waters: the

God of glory thundereth: the LORD is upon many waters.

⁴The voice of the LORD is powerful; the voice of the LORD is full of majesty.

⁵The voice of the LORD breaketh the cedars; yea, the LORD breaketh the cedars of Lebanon.

⁶He maketh them also to skip like a calf; Lebanon and Sirion like a young unicorn.

⁷The voice of the LORD divideth the flames of fire.

⁸The voice of the LORD shaketh the wilderness; the LORD shaketh the wilderness of Kadesh.

⁹The voice of the LORD maketh the hinds to calve, and discovereth the forests: and in his temple doth every one speak of his glory.

¹⁰The LORD sitteth upon the flood; yea, the LORD sitteth King for ever.

¹¹The LORD will give strength unto his people; the LORD will bless his people with peace.

## PSALM 31

*In spite of his condition, David continues to turn to God, who is consistently his refuge, rock, and fortress. David is a brilliant fighter and strategist, yet he realizes he can do no better in this situation than to commit himself into God's hands to avoid potential harm.*

¹In thee, O LORD, do I put my trust; let me never be ashamed: deliver me in thy righteousness.

²Bow down thine ear to me; deliver me speedily:

be thou my strong rock, for an house of defence to save me.

³For thou art my rock and my fortress; therefore for thy name's sake lead me, and guide me.

⁴Pull me out of the net that they have laid privily for me: for thou art my strength.

⁵Into thine hand I commit my spirit: thou hast redeemed me, O LORD God of truth.

⁶I have hated them that regard lying vanities: but I trust in the LORD.

⁷I will be glad and rejoice in thy mercy: for thou hast considered my trouble; thou hast known my soul in adversities;

⁸And hast not shut me up into the hand of the enemy: thou hast set my feet in a large room.

⁹Have mercy upon me, O LORD, for I am in trouble: mine eye is consumed with grief, yea, my soul and my belly.

¹⁰For my life is spent with grief, and my years with sighing: my strength faileth because of mine iniquity, and my bones are consumed.

¹¹I was a reproach among all mine enemies, but especially among my neighbours, and a fear to mine acquaintance: they that did see me without fled from me.

¹²I am forgotten as a dead man out of mind: I am like a broken vessel.

¹³For I have heard the slander of many: fear was on every side: while they took counsel together against me, they devised to take away my life.

¹⁴But I trusted in thee, O LORD: I said, Thou art my God.

¹⁵My times are in thy hand: deliver me from the hand of mine enemies, and from them that persecute me.

¹⁶Make thy face to shine upon thy servant: save me for thy mercies' sake.

¹⁷Let me not be ashamed, O Lord; for I have called upon thee: let the wicked be ashamed, and let them be silent in the grave.

¹⁸Let the lying lips be put to silence; which speak grievous things proudly and contemptuously against the righteous.

¹⁹Oh how great is thy goodness, which thou hast laid up for them that fear thee; which thou hast wrought for them that trust in thee before the sons of men!

²⁰Thou shalt hide them in the secret of thy presence from the pride of man: thou shalt keep them secretly in a pavilion from the strife of tongues.

²¹Blessed be the Lord: for he hath shewed me his marvellous kindness in a strong city.

²²For I said in my haste, I am cut off from before thine eyes: nevertheless thou heardest the voice of my supplications when I cried unto thee.

²³O love the Lord, all ye his saints: for the Lord preserveth the faithful, and plentifully rewardeth the proud doer.

²⁴Be of good courage, and he shall strengthen your heart, all ye that hope in the Lord.

*Unrepentant wicked people are left with many woes,*
*but God always provides a better option.*
*After sin, repentance, and confession, God restores*
*one's state of righteousness, enabling the person to once*
*again be pure in heart. Because of God's mercy and*
*forgiveness, the person is once again eager to rejoice.*

¹Blessed is he whose transgression is forgiven,
whose sin is covered.
²Blessed is the man unto whom the LORD
imputeth not iniquity, and in whose spirit there is
no guile.
³When I kept silence, my bones waxed old
through my roaring all the day long.
⁴For day and night thy hand was heavy upon
me: my moisture is turned into the drought of
summer. Selah.
⁵I acknowledged my sin unto thee, and mine
iniquity have I not hid. I said, I will confess my
transgressions unto the Lord; and thou forgavest
the iniquity of my sin. Selah.
⁶For this shall every one that is godly pray unto
thee in a time when thou mayest be found: surely
in the floods of great waters they shall not come
nigh unto him.
⁷Thou art my hiding place; thou shalt preserve me
from trouble; thou shalt compass me about with
songs of deliverance. Selah.
⁸I will instruct thee and teach thee in the way which
thou shalt go: I will guide thee with mine eye.

⁹Be ye not as the horse, or as the mule, which have no understanding: whose mouth must be held in with bit and bridle, lest they come near unto thee.

¹⁰Many sorrows shall be to the wicked: but he that trusteth in the LORD, mercy shall compass him about.

¹¹Be glad in the LORD, and rejoice, ye righteous: and shout for joy, all ye that are upright in heart.

## PSALM 33

*Psalm 33 is a beautiful acknowledgement of the sovereignty of God, who deserves worship and praise from His people because they can always count on His faithfulness, righteousness, justice, and love.*

¹Rejoice in the LORD, O ye righteous: for praise is comely for the upright.

²Praise the LORD with harp: sing unto him with the psaltery and an instrument of ten strings.

³Sing unto him a new song; play skilfully with a loud noise.

⁴For the word of the LORD is right; and all his works are done in truth.

⁵He loveth righteousness and judgment: the earth is full of the goodness of the LORD.

⁶By the word of the LORD were the heavens made; and all the host of them by the breath of his mouth.

⁷He gathereth the waters of the sea together as an heap: he layeth up the depth in storehouses.

⁸Let all the earth fear the LORD: let all the

inhabitants of the world stand in awe of him.

⁹For he spake, and it was done; he commanded, and it stood fast.

¹⁰The Lord bringeth the counsel of the heathen to nought: he maketh the devices of the people of none effect.

¹¹The counsel of the Lord standeth for ever, the thoughts of his heart to all generations.

¹²Blessed is the nation whose God is the Lord: and the people whom he hath chosen for his own inheritance.

¹³The Lord looketh from heaven; he beholdeth all the sons of men.

¹⁴From the place of his habitation he looketh upon all the inhabitants of the earth.

¹⁵He fashioneth their hearts alike; he considereth all their works.

¹⁶There is no king saved by the multitude of an host: a mighty man is not delivered by much strength.

¹⁷An horse is a vain thing for safety: neither shall he deliver any by his great strength.

¹⁸Behold, the eye of the Lord is upon them that fear him, upon them that hope in his mercy;

¹⁹To deliver their soul from death, and to keep them alive in famine.

²⁰Our soul waiteth for the Lord: he is our help and our shield.

²¹For our heart shall rejoice in him, because we have trusted in his holy name.

²²Let thy mercy, O Lord, be upon us, according as we hope in thee.

*Those with no other recourse can always call on God and be heard. And those who seek and receive God's help may even have a different look about them— they avoid the shame experienced by so many others, and their faces radiate with joy.*

¹I will bless the Lord at all times: his praise shall continually be in my mouth.

²My soul shall make her boast in the Lord: the humble shall hear thereof, and be glad.

³O magnify the Lord with me, and let us exalt his name together.

⁴I sought the Lord, and he heard me, and delivered me from all my fears.

⁵They looked unto him, and were lightened: and their faces were not ashamed.

⁶This poor man cried, and the Lord heard him, and saved him out of all his troubles.

⁷The angel of the Lord encampeth round about them that fear him, and delivereth them.

⁸O taste and see that the Lord is good: blessed is the man that trusteth in him.

⁹O fear the Lord, ye his saints: for there is no want to them that fear him.

¹⁰The young lions do lack, and suffer hunger: but they that seek the Lord shall not want any good thing.

¹¹Come, ye children, hearken unto me: I will teach you the fear of the Lord.

¹²What man is he that desireth life, and loveth many days, that he may see good?

¹³Keep thy tongue from evil, and thy lips from speaking guile.

¹⁴Depart from evil, and do good; seek peace, and pursue it.

¹⁵The eyes of the Lord are upon the righteous, and his ears are open unto their cry.

¹⁶The face of the Lord is against them that do evil, to cut off the remembrance of them from the earth.

¹⁷The righteous cry, and the Lord heareth, and delivereth them out of all their troubles.

¹⁸The Lord is nigh unto them that are of a broken heart; and saveth such as be of a contrite spirit.

¹⁹Many are the afflictions of the righteous: but the Lord delivereth him out of them all.

²⁰He keepeth all his bones: not one of them is broken.

²¹Evil shall slay the wicked: and they that hate the righteous shall be desolate.

²²The Lord redeemeth the soul of his servants: and none of them that trust in him shall be desolate.

# Psalm 37

*In verses 12–22, David lists a series of contrasts between righteous and wicked people. In each specific instance, given enough time, the apparent success of evildoers comes to a crashing end. The lasting effect of all that wickedness will never last. For the righteous, however, the blessings of God are both plentiful and eternal.*

¹Fret not thyself because of evildoers, neither be thou envious against the workers of iniquity.

²For they shall soon be cut down like the grass, and wither as the green herb.

³Trust in the Lord, and do good; so shalt thou dwell in the land, and verily thou shalt be fed.

⁴Delight thyself also in the Lord; and he shall give thee the desires of thine heart.

⁵Commit thy way unto the Lord; trust also in him; and he shall bring it to pass.

⁶And he shall bring forth thy righteousness as the light, and thy judgment as the noonday.

⁷Rest in the Lord, and wait patiently for him: fret not thyself because of him who prospereth in his way, because of the man who bringeth wicked devices to pass.

⁸Cease from anger, and forsake wrath: fret not thyself in any wise to do evil.

⁹For evildoers shall be cut off: but those that wait upon the Lord, they shall inherit the earth.

¹⁰For yet a little while, and the wicked shall not be: yea, thou shalt diligently consider his place, and it shall not be.

<sup>11</sup>But the meek shall inherit the earth; and shall delight themselves in the abundance of peace.

<sup>12</sup>The wicked plotteth against the just, and gnasheth upon him with his teeth.

<sup>13</sup>The Lord shall laugh at him: for he seeth that his day is coming.

<sup>14</sup>The wicked have drawn out the sword, and have bent their bow, to cast down the poor and needy, and to slay such as be of upright conversation.

<sup>15</sup>Their sword shall enter into their own heart, and their bows shall be broken.

<sup>16</sup>A little that a righteous man hath is better than the riches of many wicked.

<sup>17</sup>For the arms of the wicked shall be broken: but the Lord upholdeth the righteous.

<sup>18</sup>The Lord knoweth the days of the upright: and their inheritance shall be for ever.

<sup>19</sup>They shall not be ashamed in the evil time: and in the days of famine they shall be satisfied.

<sup>20</sup>But the wicked shall perish, and the enemies of the Lord shall be as the fat of lambs: they shall consume; into smoke shall they consume away.

<sup>21</sup>The wicked borroweth, and payeth not again: but the righteous sheweth mercy, and giveth.

<sup>22</sup>For such as be blessed of him shall inherit the earth; and they that be cursed of him shall be cut off.

<sup>23</sup>The steps of a good man are ordered by the Lord: and he delighteth in his way.

<sup>24</sup>Though he fall, he shall not be utterly cast down: for the Lord upholdeth him with his hand.

<sup>25</sup>I have been young, and now am old; yet have

I not seen the righteous forsaken, nor his seed begging bread.

<sup>26</sup>He is ever merciful, and lendeth; and his seed is blessed.

<sup>27</sup>Depart from evil, and do good; and dwell for evermore.

<sup>28</sup>For the LORD loveth judgment, and forsaketh not his saints; they are preserved for ever: but the seed of the wicked shall be cut off.

<sup>29</sup>The righteous shall inherit the land, and dwell therein for ever.

<sup>30</sup>The mouth of the righteous speaketh wisdom, and his tongue talketh of judgment.

<sup>31</sup>The law of his God is in his heart; none of his steps shall slide.

<sup>32</sup>The wicked watcheth the righteous, and seeketh to slay him.

<sup>33</sup>The LORD will not leave him in his hand, nor condemn him when he is judged.

<sup>34</sup>Wait on the LORD, and keep his way, and he shall exalt thee to inherit the land: when the wicked are cut off, thou shalt see it.

<sup>35</sup>I have seen the wicked in great power, and spreading himself like a green bay tree.

<sup>36</sup>Yet he passed away, and, lo, he was not: yea, I sought him, but he could not be found.

<sup>37</sup>Mark the perfect man, and behold the upright: for the end of that man is peace.

<sup>38</sup>But the transgressors shall be destroyed together: the end of the wicked shall be cut off.

<sup>39</sup>But the salvation of the righteous is of the LORD: he is their strength in the time of trouble.

⁴⁰And the LORD shall help them and deliver them: he shall deliver them from the wicked, and save them, because they trust in him.

## PSALM 39

*Turning his attention back to God, David affirms his hope in the Lord while asking to avoid being ridiculed by foolish people. Because each person's life is brief, David wants to restore his relationship with God as quickly as possible.*

¹I said, I will take heed to my ways, that I sin not with my tongue: I will keep my mouth with a bridle, while the wicked is before me.
²I was dumb with silence, I held my peace, even from good; and my sorrow was stirred.
³My heart was hot within me, while I was musing the fire burned: then spake I with my tongue,
⁴LORD, make me to know mine end, and the measure of my days, what it is; that I may know how frail I am.
⁵Behold, thou hast made my days as an handbreadth; and mine age is as nothing before thee: verily every man at his best state is altogether vanity. Selah.
⁶Surely every man walketh in a vain shew: surely they are disquieted in vain: he heapeth up riches, and knoweth not who shall gather them.
⁷And now, Lord, what wait I for? my hope is in thee.
⁸Deliver me from all my transgressions: make me

not the reproach of the foolish.

⁹I was dumb, I opened not my mouth; because thou didst it.

¹⁰Remove thy stroke away from me: I am consumed by the blow of thine hand.

¹¹When thou with rebukes dost correct man for iniquity, thou makest his beauty to consume away like a moth: surely every man is vanity. Selah.

¹²Hear my prayer, O Lord, and give ear unto my cry; hold not thy peace at my tears: for I am a stranger with thee, and a sojourner, as all my fathers were.

¹³O spare me, that I may recover strength, before I go hence, and be no more.

## Psalm 40

*God is not impressed by the outward practice of one's religion—sacrifices, offerings, and such. David realizes that the Lord far prefers a strong relationship where His Word motivates an ongoing desire to obey and respond to Him.*

¹I waited patiently for the Lord; and he inclined unto me, and heard my cry.

²He brought me up also out of an horrible pit, out of the miry clay, and set my feet upon a rock, and established my goings.

³And he hath put a new song in my mouth, even praise unto our God: many shall see it, and fear, and shall trust in the Lord.

⁴Blessed is that man that maketh the Lord his

trust, and respecteth not the proud, nor such as turn aside to lies.

⁵Many, O Lord my God, are thy wonderful works which thou hast done, and thy thoughts which are to us-ward: they cannot be reckoned up in order unto thee: if I would declare and speak of them, they are more than can be numbered.

⁶Sacrifice and offering thou didst not desire; mine ears hast thou opened: burnt offering and sin offering hast thou not required.

⁷Then said I, Lo, I come: in the volume of the book it is written of me,

⁸I delight to do thy will, O my God: yea, thy law is within my heart.

⁹I have preached righteousness in the great congregation: lo, I have not refrained my lips, O Lord, thou knowest.

¹⁰I have not hid thy righteousness within my heart; I have declared thy faithfulness and thy salvation: I have not concealed thy lovingkindness and thy truth from the great congregation.

¹¹Withhold not thou thy tender mercies from me, O Lord: let thy lovingkindness and thy truth continually preserve me.

¹²For innumerable evils have compassed me about: mine iniquities have taken hold upon me, so that I am not able to look up; they are more than the hairs of mine head: therefore my heart faileth me.

¹³Be pleased, O Lord, to deliver me: O Lord, make haste to help me.

¹⁴Let them be ashamed and confounded together

that seek after my soul to destroy it; let them be
driven backward and put to shame that wish me evil.
¹⁵Let them be desolate for a reward of their
shame that say unto me, Aha, aha.
¹⁶Let all those that seek thee rejoice and be
glad in thee: let such as love thy salvation say
continually, The Lord be magnified.
¹⁷But I am poor and needy; yet the Lord thinketh
upon me: thou art my help and my deliverer;
make no tarrying, O my God.

## PSALM 42

*Verse 4 points out that the psalmist has been prevented
not only from attending worship services but also
from taking part in his regular ministry there.
Isolation and weeping have replaced
fellowship, joy, and thanksgiving.
Yet in the first of three identical choruses, he chides
himself to overcome his negative mindset
and instead place his hope in God.*

¹As the hart panteth after the water brooks, so
panteth my soul after thee, O God.
²My soul thirsteth for God, for the living God:
when shall I come and appear before God?
³My tears have been my meat day and night,
while they continually say unto me, Where is thy
God?
⁴When I remember these things, I pour out my
soul in me: for I had gone with the multitude, I
went with them to the house of God, with the

voice of joy and praise, with a multitude that kept holyday.

⁵Why art thou cast down, O my soul? and why art thou disquieted in me? hope thou in God: for I shall yet praise him for the help of his countenance.

⁶O my God, my soul is cast down within me: therefore will I remember thee from the land of Jordan, and of the Hermonites, from the hill Mizar.

⁷Deep calleth unto deep at the noise of thy waterspouts: all thy waves and thy billows are gone over me.

⁸Yet the LORD will command his lovingkindness in the day time, and in the night his song shall be with me, and my prayer unto the God of my life.

⁹I will say unto God my rock, Why hast thou forgotten me? why go I mourning because of the oppression of the enemy?

¹⁰As with a sword in my bones, mine enemies reproach me; while they say daily unto me, Where is thy God?

¹¹Why art thou cast down, O my soul? and why art thou disquieted within me? hope thou in God: for I shall yet praise him, who is the health of my countenance, and my God.

*In the original language, the instruction to "Be still, and know that I am God" is less a suggestion than an emphatic command. The intent is not, "Quiet down and you'll discover God's presence," but rather, "Quit what you're doing right now and acknowledge who God is."*

¹God is our refuge and strength, a very present help in trouble.

²Therefore will not we fear, though the earth be removed, and though the mountains be carried into the midst of the sea;

³Though the waters thereof roar and be troubled, though the mountains shake with the swelling thereof. Selah.

⁴There is a river, the streams whereof shall make glad the city of God, the holy place of the tabernacles of the most High.

⁵God is in the midst of her; she shall not be moved: God shall help her, and that right early.

⁶The heathen raged, the kingdoms were moved: he uttered his voice, the earth melted.

⁷The LORD of hosts is with us; the God of Jacob is our refuge. Selah.

⁸Come, behold the works of the LORD, what desolations he hath made in the earth.

⁹He maketh wars to cease unto the end of the earth; he breaketh the bow, and cutteth the spear in sunder; he burneth the chariot in the fire.

¹⁰Be still, and know that I am God: I will be exalted among the heathen, I will be exalted in the earth.

¹¹The Lord of hosts is with us; the God of Jacob is our refuge. Selah.

## Psalm 47

*While Psalm 46 focuses exclusively on Israel, Psalm 47 immediately makes clear in the opening verse that God is to be acknowledged by all the nations. Indeed, Israel's God is both the Lord Most High and the great King over all the earth.*

¹O clap your hands, all ye people; shout unto God with the voice of triumph.

²For the Lord most high is terrible; he is a great King over all the earth.

³He shall subdue the people under us, and the nations under our feet.

⁴He shall choose our inheritance for us, the excellency of Jacob whom he loved. Selah.

⁵God is gone up with a shout, the Lord with the sound of a trumpet.

⁶Sing praises to God, sing praises: sing praises unto our King, sing praises.

⁷For God is the King of all the earth: sing ye praises with understanding.

⁸God reigneth over the heathen: God sitteth upon the throne of his holiness.

⁹The princes of the people are gathered together, even the people of the God of Abraham: for the shields of the earth belong unto God: he is greatly exalted.

*Psalm 49 addresses a recurring theme: the apparent
injustice of life as the rich dominate the poor.
The psalmist will put things in perspective, however,
by explaining that death is the great equalizer.
No matter how rich or wise a person might be,
there is no escaping the same inevitable end
as the poor and the foolish.*

¹Hear this, all ye people; give ear, all ye
inhabitants of the world:
²Both low and high, rich and poor, together.
³My mouth shall speak of wisdom; and the
meditation of my heart shall be of understanding.
⁴I will incline mine ear to a parable: I will open
my dark saying upon the harp.
⁵Wherefore should I fear in the days of evil, when
the iniquity of my heels shall compass me about?
⁶They that trust in their wealth, and boast
themselves in the multitude of their riches;
⁷None of them can by any means redeem his
brother, nor give to God a ransom for him:
⁸(For the redemption of their soul is precious, and
it ceaseth for ever:)
⁹That he should still live for ever, and not see
corruption.
¹⁰For he seeth that wise men die, likewise the fool
and the brutish person perish, and leave their
wealth to others.
¹¹Their inward thought is, that their houses shall
continue for ever, and their dwelling places to all
generations; they call their lands after their own
names.

¹²Nevertheless man being in honour abideth not: he is like the beasts that perish.

¹³This their way is their folly: yet their posterity approve their sayings. Selah.

¹⁴Like sheep they are laid in the grave; death shall feed on them; and the upright shall have dominion over them in the morning; and their beauty shall consume in the grave from their dwelling.

¹⁵But God will redeem my soul from the power of the grave: for he shall receive me. Selah.

¹⁶Be not thou afraid when one is made rich, when the glory of his house is increased;

¹⁷For when he dieth he shall carry nothing away: his glory shall not descend after him.

¹⁸Though while he lived he blessed his soul: and men will praise thee, when thou doest well to thyself.

¹⁹He shall go to the generation of his fathers; they shall never see light.

²⁰Man that is in honour, and understandeth not, is like the beasts that perish.

*David prays not only for a pure heart
but also for a steadfast spirit and ongoing
awareness of God's presence.
After his grievous sin, he desires the joy of salvation
and a renewal of his willingness to serve God.*

¹Have mercy upon me, O God, according to thy
lovingkindness: according unto the multitude of
thy tender mercies blot out my transgressions.
²Wash me throughly from mine iniquity, and
cleanse me from my sin.
³For I acknowledge my transgressions: and my sin
is ever before me.
⁴Against thee, thee only, have I sinned, and
done this evil in thy sight: that thou mightest be
justified when thou speakest, and be clear when
thou judgest.
⁵Behold, I was shapen in iniquity; and in sin did
my mother conceive me.
⁶Behold, thou desirest truth in the inward parts:
and in the hidden part thou shalt make me to
know wisdom.
⁷Purge me with hyssop, and I shall be clean: wash
me, and I shall be whiter than snow.
⁸Make me to hear joy and gladness; that the
bones which thou hast broken may rejoice.
⁹Hide thy face from my sins, and blot out all mine
iniquities.
¹⁰Create in me a clean heart, O God; and renew a
right spirit within me.
¹¹Cast me not away from thy presence; and take

not thy holy spirit from me.

¹²Restore unto me the joy of thy salvation; and uphold me with thy free spirit.

¹³Then will I teach transgressors thy ways; and sinners shall be converted unto thee.

¹⁴Deliver me from bloodguiltiness, O God, thou God of my salvation: and my tongue shall sing aloud of thy righteousness.

¹⁵O Lord, open thou my lips; and my mouth shall shew forth thy praise.

¹⁶For thou desirest not sacrifice; else would I give it: thou delightest not in burnt offering.

¹⁷The sacrifices of God are a broken spirit: a broken and a contrite heart, O God, thou wilt not despise.

¹⁸Do good in thy good pleasure unto Zion: build thou the walls of Jerusalem.

¹⁹Then shalt thou be pleased with the sacrifices of righteousness, with burnt offering and whole burnt offering: then shall they offer bullocks upon thine altar.

# Psalm 52

*In contrast to the wicked, who will be uprooted,*
*in verse 8 David compares himself to an olive tree—*
*securely rooted, productive, and anticipating long life.*
*(Olive trees can live for centuries.) More importantly,*
*he is flourishing in his relationship with God.*
*His trust in God makes all the difference, and he*
*promises to continue to praise the Lord*
*and place his hope in Him.*

¹Why boastest thou thyself in mischief, O mighty man? the goodness of God endureth continually.
²Thy tongue deviseth mischiefs; like a sharp razor, working deceitfully.
³Thou lovest evil more than good; and lying rather than to speak righteousness. Selah.
⁴Thou lovest all devouring words, O thou deceitful tongue.
⁵God shall likewise destroy thee for ever, he shall take thee away, and pluck thee out of thy dwelling place, and root thee out of the land of the living. Selah.
⁶The righteous also shall see, and fear, and shall laugh at him:
⁷Lo, this is the man that made not God his strength; but trusted in the abundance of his riches, and strengthened himself in his wickedness.
⁸But I am like a green olive tree in the house of God: I trust in the mercy of God for ever and ever.
⁹I will praise thee for ever, because thou hast done it: and I will wait on thy name; for it is good before thy saints.

# PSALM 57

*Disasters will come and go, and during the
worst of times the best place to be is in the shadow
of God's wings. Saul's army is pursuing David,
but he is also being followed
by God's love and faithfulness.*

[1]Be merciful unto me, O God, be merciful unto me: for my soul trusteth in thee: yea, in the shadow of thy wings will I make my refuge, until these calamities be overpast.

[2]I will cry unto God most high; unto God that performeth all things for me.

[3]He shall send from heaven, and save me from the reproach of him that would swallow me up. Selah. God shall send forth his mercy and his truth.

[4]My soul is among lions: and I lie even among them that are set on fire, even the sons of men, whose teeth are spears and arrows, and their tongue a sharp sword.

[5]Be thou exalted, O God, above the heavens; let thy glory be above all the earth.

[6]They have prepared a net for my steps; my soul is bowed down: they have digged a pit before me, into the midst whereof they are fallen themselves. Selah.

[7]My heart is fixed, O God, my heart is fixed: I will sing and give praise.

[8]Awake up, my glory; awake, psaltery and harp: I myself will awake early.

[9]I will praise thee, O Lord, among the people: I

will sing unto thee among the nations.

¹⁰For thy mercy is great unto the heavens, and thy truth unto the clouds.

¹¹Be thou exalted, O God, above the heavens: let thy glory be above all the earth.

## PSALM 61

*In verse 3, the psalmist is able to trust God during this crisis because God has always been faithful in previous times of trouble. He desires a more permanent sense of closeness to God with the protection of both the sanctuary of God and the Lord's personal presence.*

¹Hear my cry, O God; attend unto my prayer.

²From the end of the earth will I cry unto thee, when my heart is overwhelmed: lead me to the rock that is higher than I.

³For thou hast been a shelter for me, and a strong tower from the enemy.

⁴I will abide in thy tabernacle for ever: I will trust in the covert of thy wings. Selah.

⁵For thou, O God, hast heard my vows: thou hast given me the heritage of those that fear thy name.

⁶Thou wilt prolong the king's life: and his years as many generations.

⁷He shall abide before God for ever: O prepare mercy and truth, which may preserve him.

⁸So will I sing praise unto thy name for ever, that I may daily perform my vows.

# Psalm 62

*People tend to pursue riches, and many desperately turn to dishonest means (including stealing and extortion) to acquire wealth. Yet a person's accumulated possessions provide no long-range security. One's heart should remain on God, not any other substitute.*

[1]Truly my soul waiteth upon God: from him cometh my salvation.

[2]He only is my rock and my salvation; he is my defence; I shall not be greatly moved.

[3]How long will ye imagine mischief against a man? ye shall be slain all of you: as a bowing wall shall ye be, and as a tottering fence.

[4]They only consult to cast him down from his excellency: they delight in lies: they bless with their mouth, but they curse inwardly. Selah.

[5]My soul, wait thou only upon God; for my expectation is from him.

[6]He only is my rock and my salvation: he is my defence; I shall not be moved.

[7]In God is my salvation and my glory: the rock of my strength, and my refuge, is in God.

[8]Trust in him at all times; ye people, pour out your heart before him: God is a refuge for us. Selah.

[9]Surely men of low degree are vanity, and men of high degree are a lie: to be laid in the balance, they are altogether lighter than vanity.

[10]Trust not in oppression, and become not vain in robbery: if riches increase, set not your heart upon them.

¹¹God hath spoken once; twice have I heard this;
that power belongeth unto God.
¹²Also unto thee, O Lord, belongeth mercy: for
thou renderest to every man according to his work.

## PSALM 63

*In verse 1, David compares his longing for God to
the thirst of a man wandering in a dry wilderness,
desperate for water. For many people, the desire for
God is a casual and occasional thing;
for David, it is a matter of life and death.*

¹O God, thou art my God; early will I seek thee:
my soul thirsteth for thee, my flesh longeth for
thee in a dry and thirsty land, where no water is;
²To see thy power and thy glory, so as I have seen
thee in the sanctuary.
³Because thy lovingkindness is better than life, my
lips shall praise thee.
⁴Thus will I bless thee while I live: I will lift up
my hands in thy name.
⁵My soul shall be satisfied as with marrow and
fatness; and my mouth shall praise thee with
joyful lips:
⁶When I remember thee upon my bed, and
meditate on thee in the night watches.
⁷Because thou hast been my help, therefore in the
shadow of thy wings will I rejoice.
⁸My soul followeth hard after thee: thy right hand
upholdeth me.
⁹But those that seek my soul, to destroy it, shall

go into the lower parts of the earth.

[10]They shall fall by the sword: they shall be a portion for foxes.

[11]But the king shall rejoice in God; every one that sweareth by him shall glory: but the mouth of them that speak lies shall be stopped.

## PSALM 65

*God's control extends to the farthest seas and the mighty mountains of the world, as well as the chaos among the nations. Go far enough in one direction, the psalmist realizes, and the sun is coming up. Face the other direction and go far enough, and the sun is setting. Throughout that entire span, the people should notice and revere the works of God, and they should respond in joy.*

[1]Praise waiteth for thee, O God, in Sion: and unto thee shall the vow be performed.

[2]O thou that hearest prayer, unto thee shall all flesh come.

[3]Iniquities prevail against me: as for our transgressions, thou shalt purge them away.

[4]Blessed is the man whom thou choosest, and causest to approach unto thee, that he may dwell in thy courts: we shall be satisfied with the goodness of thy house, even of thy holy temple.

[5]By terrible things in righteousness wilt thou answer us, O God of our salvation; who art the confidence of all the ends of the earth, and of them that are afar off upon the sea:

⁶Which by his strength setteth fast the mountains; being girded with power:

⁷Which stilleth the noise of the seas, the noise of their waves, and the tumult of the people.

⁸They also that dwell in the uttermost parts are afraid at thy tokens: thou makest the outgoings of the morning and evening to rejoice.

⁹Thou visitest the earth, and waterest it: thou greatly enrichest it with the river of God, which is full of water: thou preparest them corn, when thou hast so provided for it.

¹⁰Thou waterest the ridges thereof abundantly: thou settlest the furrows thereof: thou makest it soft with showers: thou blessest the springing thereof.

¹¹Thou crownest the year with thy goodness; and thy paths drop fatness.

¹²They drop upon the pastures of the wilderness: and the little hills rejoice on every side.

¹³The pastures are clothed with flocks; the valleys also are covered over with corn; they shout for joy, they also sing.

# PSALM 66

*The psalmist's people had been through some difficult times, including prison, defeat, and other trials. But rather than being brought down by such experiences, the psalmist realizes that they have merely been refined, as when precious metal is treated with intense heat in order to remove any impurities.*

¹Make a joyful noise unto God, all ye lands:
²Sing forth the honour of his name: make his praise glorious.
³Say unto God, How terrible art thou in thy works! through the greatness of thy power shall thine enemies submit themselves unto thee.
⁴All the earth shall worship thee, and shall sing unto thee; they shall sing to thy name. Selah.
⁵Come and see the works of God: he is terrible in his doing toward the children of men.
⁶He turned the sea into dry land: they went through the flood on foot: there did we rejoice in him.
⁷He ruleth by his power for ever; his eyes behold the nations: let not the rebellious exalt themselves. Selah.
⁸O bless our God, ye people, and make the voice of his praise to be heard:
⁹Which holdeth our soul in life, and suffereth not our feet to be moved.
¹⁰For thou, O God, hast proved us: thou hast tried us, as silver is tried.
¹¹Thou broughtest us into the net; thou laidst affliction upon our loins.

<sup>12</sup>Thou hast caused men to ride over our heads; we went through fire and through water: but thou broughtest us out into a wealthy place.

<sup>13</sup>I will go into thy house with burnt offerings: I will pay thee my vows,

<sup>14</sup>Which my lips have uttered, and my mouth hath spoken, when I was in trouble.

<sup>15</sup>I will offer unto thee burnt sacrifices of fatlings, with the incense of rams; I will offer bullocks with goats. Selah.

<sup>16</sup>Come and hear, all ye that fear God, and I will declare what he hath done for my soul.

<sup>17</sup>I cried unto him with my mouth, and he was extolled with my tongue.

<sup>18</sup>If I regard iniquity in my heart, the Lord will not hear me:

<sup>19</sup>But verily God hath heard me; he hath attended to the voice of my prayer.

<sup>20</sup>Blessed be God, which hath not turned away my prayer, nor his mercy from me.

# PSALM 67

*Ideally, praise will not be confined within Israel.*
*In verses 3–4, the psalmist wants all the nations to*
*praise God, who is a just ruler of people and a guide*
*for all the countries. And if the psalmist's initial*
*invitation isn't enough, he repeats it again in verse 5.*

[1]God be merciful unto us, and bless us; and cause his face to shine upon us; Selah.
[2]That thy way may be known upon earth, thy saving health among all nations.
[3]Let the people praise thee, O God; let all the people praise thee.
[4]O let the nations be glad and sing for joy: for thou shalt judge the people righteously, and govern the nations upon earth. Selah.
[5]Let the people praise thee, O God; let all the people praise thee.
[6]Then shall the earth yield her increase; and God, even our own God, shall bless us.
[7]God shall bless us; and all the ends of the earth shall fear him.

*Speaking with the wisdom of age, the psalmist
continues to place his hope in God. He had not yet
discovered the full extent of God's righteousness and
salvation, but he had seen more than enough
to proclaim God's goodness to others.*

¹In thee, O LORD, do I put my trust: let me never
be put to confusion.

²Deliver me in thy righteousness, and cause me to
escape: incline thine ear unto me, and save me.

³Be thou my strong habitation, whereunto I may
continually resort: thou hast given commandment
to save me; for thou art my rock and my fortress.

⁴Deliver me, O my God, out of the hand of the
wicked, out of the hand of the unrighteous and
cruel man.

⁵For thou art my hope, O Lord GOD: thou art my
trust from my youth.

⁶By thee have I been holden up from the womb:
thou art he that took me out of my mother's
bowels: my praise shall be continually of thee.

⁷I am as a wonder unto many; but thou art my
strong refuge.

⁸Let my mouth be filled with thy praise and with
thy honour all the day.

⁹Cast me not off in the time of old age; forsake
me not when my strength faileth.

¹⁰For mine enemies speak against me; and they
that lay wait for my soul take counsel together,

¹¹Saying, God hath forsaken him: persecute and
take him; for there is none to deliver him.

¹²O God, be not far from me: O my God, make haste for my help.

¹³Let them be confounded and consumed that are adversaries to my soul; let them be covered with reproach and dishonour that seek my hurt.

¹⁴But I will hope continually, and will yet praise thee more and more.

¹⁵My mouth shall shew forth thy righteousness and thy salvation all the day; for I know not the numbers thereof.

¹⁶I will go in the strength of the Lord GOD: I will make mention of thy righteousness, even of thine only.

¹⁷O God, thou hast taught me from my youth: and hitherto have I declared thy wondrous works.

¹⁸Now also when I am old and greyheaded, O God, forsake me not; until I have shewed thy strength unto this generation, and thy power to every one that is to come.

¹⁹Thy righteousness also, O God, is very high, who hast done great things: O God, who is like unto thee!

²⁰Thou, which hast shewed me great and sore troubles, shalt quicken me again, and shalt bring me up again from the depths of the earth.

²¹Thou shalt increase my greatness, and comfort me on every side.

²²I will also praise thee with the psaltery, even thy truth, O my God: unto thee will I sing with the harp, O thou Holy One of Israel.

²³My lips shall greatly rejoice when I sing unto thee; and my soul, which thou hast redeemed.

24My tongue also shall talk of thy righteousness all the day long: for they are confounded, for they are brought unto shame, that seek my hurt.

## PSALM 75

*The connection between the nearness of God's name
and people telling of His deeds
can be understood in two ways. Perhaps it means that
those who worship the name of God
naturally begin to talk about the great things He has
done. Or it may be the other way around:
As people recall the wonderful deeds of God, they can't
help but give thanks that He remains so near.*

1Unto thee, O God, do we give thanks, unto thee do we give thanks: for that thy name is near thy wondrous works declare.

2When I shall receive the congregation I will judge uprightly.

3The earth and all the inhabitants thereof are dissolved: I bear up the pillars of it. Selah.

4I said unto the fools, Deal not foolishly: and to the wicked, Lift not up the horn:

5Lift not up your horn on high: speak not with a stiff neck.

6For promotion cometh neither from the east, nor from the west, nor from the south.

7But God is the judge: he putteth down one, and setteth up another.

8For in the hand of the LORD there is a cup, and the wine is red; it is full of mixture; and he poureth out of the same: but the dregs thereof, all the wicked of the earth shall wring them out, and drink them.

⁹But I will declare for ever; I will sing praises to the God of Jacob.

¹⁰All the horns of the wicked also will I cut off; but the horns of the righteous shall be exalted.

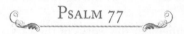

## PSALM 77

*With renewed enthusiasm, the psalmist begins to recall one of God's greatest deliverances: the Exodus of the Hebrew people from Egypt. Beyond a doubt, God had been with His people. Therefore, any doubts about God are unfounded. He is still a God of power and love who will deliver His people.*

¹I cried unto God with my voice, even unto God with my voice; and he gave ear unto me.

²In the day of my trouble I sought the Lord: my sore ran in the night, and ceased not: my soul refused to be comforted.

³I remembered God, and was troubled: I complained, and my spirit was overwhelmed. Selah.

⁴Thou holdest mine eyes waking: I am so troubled that I cannot speak.

⁵I have considered the days of old, the years of ancient times.

⁶I call to remembrance my song in the night: I commune with mine own heart: and my spirit

made diligent search.

⁷Will the Lord cast off for ever? and will he be favourable no more?

⁸Is his mercy clean gone for ever? doth his promise fail for evermore?

⁹Hath God forgotten to be gracious? hath he in anger shut up his tender mercies? Selah.

¹⁰And I said, This is my infirmity: but I will remember the years of the right hand of the most High.

¹¹I will remember the works of the LORD: surely I will remember thy wonders of old.

¹²I will meditate also of all thy work, and talk of thy doings.

¹³Thy way, O God, is in the sanctuary: who is so great a God as our God?

¹⁴Thou art the God that doest wonders: thou hast declared thy strength among the people.

¹⁵Thou hast with thine arm redeemed thy people, the sons of Jacob and Joseph. Selah.

¹⁶The waters saw thee, O God, the waters saw thee; they were afraid: the depths also were troubled.

¹⁷The clouds poured out water: the skies sent out a sound: thine arrows also went abroad.

¹⁸The voice of thy thunder was in the heaven: the lightnings lightened the world: the earth trembled and shook.

¹⁹Thy way is in the sea, and thy path in the great waters, and thy footsteps are not known.

²⁰Thou leddest thy people like a flock by the hand of Moses and Aaron.

*After someone has experienced a rich and rewarding
relationship with God,
it changes the person's perspective on life.
Psalm 84 is an expression of longing by the psalmist to
be closer to God and remain close.
The opening verses appear to focus
on the temple building with its courts,
yet by the end of the psalm it becomes clear that it is
the presence of God Himself that the writer desires.*

¹How amiable are thy tabernacles, O Lᴏʀᴅ of hosts!

²My soul longeth, yea, even fainteth for the courts of the Lᴏʀᴅ: my heart and my flesh crieth out for the living God.

³Yea, the sparrow hath found an house, and the swallow a nest for herself, where she may lay her young, even thine altars, O Lᴏʀᴅ of hosts, my King, and my God.

⁴Blessed are they that dwell in thy house: they will be still praising thee. Selah.

⁵Blessed is the man whose strength is in thee; in whose heart are the ways of them.

⁶Who passing through the valley of Baca make it a well; the rain also filleth the pools.

⁷They go from strength to strength, every one of them in Zion appeareth before God.

⁸O Lᴏʀᴅ God of hosts, hear my prayer: give ear, O God of Jacob. Selah.

⁹Behold, O God our shield, and look upon the face of thine anointed.

<sup>10</sup>For a day in thy courts is better than a thousand. I had rather be a doorkeeper in the house of my God, than to dwell in the tents of wickedness.
<sup>11</sup>For the LORD God is a sun and shield: the LORD will give grace and glory: no good thing will he withhold from them that walk uprightly.
<sup>12</sup>O LORD of hosts, blessed is the man that trusteth in thee.

## PSALM 86

*Since God has been slow to become
angry with David in the past,
perhaps the psalmist can understand why
God doesn't immediately condemn others
who are behaving sinfully. Therefore,
rather than ask for his enemies' quick demise,
David asks God to do something good for
him that they will see—and perhaps
shame them into repentance.
In the meantime, David counts on God's strength,
deliverance, help, and comfort.*

<sup>1</sup>Bow down thine ear, O LORD, hear me: for I am poor and needy.
<sup>2</sup>Preserve my soul; for I am holy: O thou my God, save thy servant that trusteth in thee.
<sup>3</sup>Be merciful unto me, O Lord: for I cry unto thee daily.
<sup>4</sup>Rejoice the soul of thy servant: for unto thee, O Lord, do I lift up my soul.
<sup>5</sup>For thou, Lord, art good, and ready to forgive; and plenteous in mercy unto all them that call

upon thee.

⁶Give ear, O LORD, unto my prayer; and attend to the voice of my supplications.

⁷In the day of my trouble I will call upon thee: for thou wilt answer me.

⁸Among the gods there is none like unto thee, O Lord; neither are there any works like unto thy works.

⁹All nations whom thou hast made shall come and worship before thee, O Lord; and shall glorify thy name.

¹⁰For thou art great, and doest wondrous things: thou art God alone.

¹¹Teach me thy way, O LORD; I will walk in thy truth: unite my heart to fear thy name.

¹²I will praise thee, O LORD my God, with all my heart: and I will glorify thy name for evermore.

¹³For great is thy mercy toward me: and thou hast delivered my soul from the lowest hell.

¹⁴O God, the proud are risen against me, and the assemblies of violent men have sought after my soul; and have not set thee before them.

¹⁵But thou, O Lord, art a God full of compassion, and gracious, long suffering, and plenteous in mercy and truth.

¹⁶O turn unto me, and have mercy upon me; give thy strength unto thy servant, and save the son of thine handmaid.

¹⁷Shew me a token for good; that they which hate me may see it, and be ashamed: because thou, LORD, hast holpen me, and comforted me.

# Psalm 89

*The positive message of verse 52 is not part of the psalm. This final verse is a doxology inserted as a conclusion for Book III. Following the lament that ends Psalm 89, it is a welcome addition.*

¹I will sing of the mercies of the LORD for ever: with my mouth will I make known thy faithfulness to all generations.

²For I have said, Mercy shall be built up for ever: thy faithfulness shalt thou establish in the very heavens.

³I have made a covenant with my chosen, I have sworn unto David my servant,

⁴Thy seed will I establish for ever, and build up thy throne to all generations. Selah.

⁵And the heavens shall praise thy wonders, O LORD: thy faithfulness also in the congregation of the saints.

⁶For who in the heaven can be compared unto the LORD? who among the sons of the mighty can be likened unto the LORD?

⁷God is greatly to be feared in the assembly of the saints, and to be had in reverence of all them that are about him.

⁸O LORD God of hosts, who is a strong LORD like unto thee? or to thy faithfulness round about thee?

⁹Thou rulest the raging of the sea: when the waves thereof arise, thou stillest them.

¹⁰Thou hast broken Rahab in pieces, as one that is slain; thou hast scattered thine enemies with thy strong arm.

¹¹The heavens are thine, the earth also is thine: as for the world and the fulness thereof, thou hast founded them.

¹²The north and the south thou hast created them: Tabor and Hermon shall rejoice in thy name.

¹³Thou hast a mighty arm: strong is thy hand, and high is thy right hand.

¹⁴Justice and judgment are the habitation of thy throne: mercy and truth shall go before thy face.

¹⁵Blessed is the people that know the joyful sound: they shall walk, O LORD, in the light of thy countenance.

¹⁶In thy name shall they rejoice all the day: and in thy righteousness shall they be exalted.

¹⁷For thou art the glory of their strength: and in thy favour our horn shall be exalted.

¹⁸For the LORD is our defence; and the Holy One of Israel is our king.

¹⁹Then thou spakest in vision to thy holy one, and saidst, I have laid help upon one that is mighty; I have exalted one chosen out of the people.

²⁰I have found David my servant; with my holy oil have I anointed him:

²¹With whom my hand shall be established: mine arm also shall strengthen him.

²²The enemy shall not exact upon him; nor the son of wickedness afflict him.

²³And I will beat down his foes before his face, and plague them that hate him.

²⁴But my faithfulness and my mercy shall be with him: and in my name shall his horn be exalted.

²⁵I will set his hand also in the sea, and his right

hand in the rivers.

²⁶He shall cry unto me, Thou art my father, my God, and the rock of my salvation.

²⁷Also I will make him my firstborn, higher than the kings of the earth.

²⁸My mercy will I keep for him for evermore, and my covenant shall stand fast with him.

²⁹His seed also will I make to endure for ever, and his throne as the days of heaven.

³⁰If his children forsake my law, and walk not in my judgments;

³¹If they break my statutes, and keep not my commandments;

³²Then will I visit their transgression with the rod, and their iniquity with stripes.

³³Nevertheless my lovingkindness will I not utterly take from him, nor suffer my faithfulness to fail.

³⁴My covenant will I not break, nor alter the thing that is gone out of my lips.

³⁵Once have I sworn by my holiness that I will not lie unto David.

³⁶His seed shall endure for ever, and his throne as the sun before me.

³⁷It shall be established for ever as the moon, and as a faithful witness in heaven. Selah.

³⁸But thou hast cast off and abhorred, thou hast been wroth with thine anointed.

³⁹Thou hast made void the covenant of thy servant: thou hast profaned his crown by casting it to the ground.

⁴⁰Thou hast broken down all his hedges; thou hast

brought his strong holds to ruin.

⁴¹All that pass by the way spoil him: he is a reproach to his neighbours.

⁴²Thou hast set up the right hand of his adversaries; thou hast made all his enemies to rejoice.

⁴³Thou hast also turned the edge of his sword, and hast not made him to stand in the battle.

⁴⁴Thou hast made his glory to cease, and cast his throne down to the ground.

⁴⁵The days of his youth hast thou shortened: thou hast covered him with shame. Selah.

⁴⁶How long, Lord? wilt thou hide thyself for ever? shall thy wrath burn like fire?

⁴⁷Remember how short my time is: wherefore hast thou made all men in vain?

⁴⁸What man is he that liveth, and shall not see death? shall he deliver his soul from the hand of the grave? Selah.

⁴⁹Lord, where are thy former lovingkindnesses, which thou swarest unto David in thy truth?

⁵⁰Remember, Lord, the reproach of thy servants; how I do bear in my bosom the reproach of all the mighty people;

⁵¹Wherewith thine enemies have reproached, O Lord; wherewith they have reproached the footsteps of thine anointed.

⁵²Blessed be the Lord for evermore. Amen, and Amen.

# PSALM 90

*If human life is but a day in the time frame of God,
then let the morning begin with God's unfailing love
that results in lasting joy and gladness.*

¹ Lord, thou hast been our dwelling place in all
generations.
²Before the mountains were brought forth, or ever
thou hadst formed the earth and the world, even
from everlasting to everlasting, thou art God.
³Thou turnest man to destruction; and sayest,
Return, ye children of men.
⁴For a thousand years in thy sight are but as yester-
day when it is past, and as a watch in the night.
⁵Thou carriest them away as with a flood; they
are as a sleep: in the morning they are like grass
which groweth up.
⁶In the morning it flourisheth, and groweth up; in
the evening it is cut down, and withereth.
⁷For we are consumed by thine anger, and by thy
wrath are we troubled.
⁸Thou hast set our iniquities before thee, our
secret sins in the light of thy countenance.
⁹For all our days are passed away in thy wrath: we
spend our years as a tale that is told.
¹⁰The days of our years are threescore years and
ten; and if by reason of strength they be fourscore
years, yet is their strength labour and sorrow; for
it is soon cut off, and we fly away.
¹¹Who knoweth the power of thine anger? even
according to thy fear, so is thy wrath.
¹²So teach us to number our days, that we may

apply our hearts unto wisdom.

¹³Return, O Lᴏʀᴅ, how long? and let it repent thee concerning thy servants.

¹⁴O satisfy us early with thy mercy; that we may rejoice and be glad all our days.

¹⁵Make us glad according to the days wherein thou hast afflicted us, and the years wherein we have seen evil.

¹⁶Let thy work appear unto thy servants, and thy glory unto their children.

¹⁷And let the beauty of the Lᴏʀᴅ our God be upon us: and establish thou the work of our hands upon us; yea, the work of our hands establish thou it.

## Psalm 91

*God loves people, and some choose to return His love,
prompting God's rescue and protection.
When they call on God, He answers.
When trouble strikes, He delivers them.
And as a result, such people tend to experience
longer, more satisfying lives.*

¹He that dwelleth in the secret place of the most High shall abide under the shadow of the Almighty.

²I will say of the Lᴏʀᴅ, He is my refuge and my fortress: my God; in him will I trust.

³Surely he shall deliver thee from the snare of the fowler, and from the noisome pestilence.

⁴He shall cover thee with his feathers, and under his wings shalt thou trust: his truth shall be thy

shield and buckler.

⁵Thou shalt not be afraid for the terror by night; nor for the arrow that flieth by day;

⁶Nor for the pestilence that walketh in darkness; nor for the destruction that wasteth at noonday.

⁷A thousand shall fall at thy side, and ten thousand at thy right hand; but it shall not come nigh thee.

⁸Only with thine eyes shalt thou behold and see the reward of the wicked.

⁹Because thou hast made the LORD, which is my refuge, even the most High, thy habitation;

¹⁰There shall no evil befall thee, neither shall any plague come nigh thy dwelling.

¹¹For he shall give his angels charge over thee, to keep thee in all thy ways.

¹²They shall bear thee up in their hands, lest thou dash thy foot against a stone.

¹³Thou shalt tread upon the lion and adder: the young lion and the dragon shalt thou trample under feet.

¹⁴Because he hath set his love upon me, therefore will I deliver him: I will set him on high, because he hath known my name.

¹⁵He shall call upon me, and I will answer him: I will be with him in trouble; I will deliver him, and honour him.

¹⁶With long life will I satisfy him, and shew him my salvation.

*The poetic expression of the writer can be confusing
to modern ears. The point of verse 2 is not to detach
the love of God from His faithfulness and to set aside
different times to acknowledge each one. Rather, God's
love and faithfulness are intertwined, and people should
proclaim them all the time (morning and night).*

¹IT IS A GOOD THING TO GIVE THANKS UNTO THE
LORD, AND TO SING PRAISES UNTO THY NAME, O
MOST HIGH:
²To shew forth thy lovingkindness in the
morning, and thy faithfulness every night,
³Upon an instrument of ten strings, and upon the
psaltery; upon the harp with a solemn sound.
⁴For thou, LORD, hast made me glad through thy
work: I will triumph in the works of thy hands.
⁵O LORD, how great are thy works! and thy
thoughts are very deep.
⁶A brutish man knoweth not; neither doth a fool
understand this.
⁷When the wicked spring as the grass, and when
all the workers of iniquity do flourish; it is that
they shall be destroyed for ever:
⁸But thou, LORD, art most high for evermore.
⁹For, lo, thine enemies, O LORD, for, lo, thine
enemies shall perish; all the workers of iniquity
shall be scattered.
¹⁰But my horn shalt thou exalt like the horn of an
unicorn: I shall be anointed with fresh oil.
¹¹Mine eye also shall see my desire on mine
enemies, and mine ears shall hear my desire of the

wicked that rise up against me.
<sup>12</sup>The righteous shall flourish like the palm tree:
he shall grow like a cedar in Lebanon.
<sup>13</sup>Those that be planted in the house of the LORD
shall flourish in the courts of our God.
<sup>14</sup>They shall still bring forth fruit in old age; they
shall be fat and flourishing;
<sup>15</sup>To shew that the LORD is upright: he is my rock,
and there is no unrighteousness in him.

## PSALM 93

*Regardless of the various forms of human government,
the truth of the matter is found in verse 1:
The Lord reigns. Human kings can be identified by
their clothing; God's royal clothing is His majesty.
He needs no weapon other than His own strength.
His right to rule is established from eternity—it has
always existed and always will.*

<sup>1</sup>The LORD reigneth, he is clothed with majesty;
the LORD is clothed with strength, wherewith he
hath girded himself: the world also is stablished,
that it cannot be moved.
<sup>2</sup>Thy throne is established of old: thou art from
everlasting.
<sup>3</sup>The floods have lifted up, O LORD, the floods have
lifted up their voice; the floods lift up their waves.
<sup>4</sup>The LORD on high is mightier than the noise of
many waters, yea, than the mighty waves of the sea.
<sup>5</sup>Thy testimonies are very sure: holiness becometh
thine house, O LORD, for ever.

# PSALM 95

*For anyone with a monotheistic upbringing, verses 3–6 may sound like obvious statements: God rules the heights and depths, lands and seas of the entire world. However, this concept would have been perplexing for many of the nations surrounding Israel, who had gods of the mountains, gods of the seas, and so forth.*

¹O come, let us sing unto the LORD: let us make a joyful noise to the rock of our salvation.

²Let us come before his presence with thanksgiving, and make a joyful noise unto him with psalms.

³For the LORD is a great God, and a great King above all gods.

⁴In his hand are the deep places of the earth: the strength of the hills is his also.

⁵The sea is his, and he made it: and his hands formed the dry land.

⁶O come, let us worship and bow down: let us kneel before the LORD our maker.

⁷For he is our God; and we are the people of his pasture, and the sheep of his hand. To day if ye will hear his voice,

⁸Harden not your heart, as in the provocation, and as in the day of temptation in the wilderness:

⁹When your fathers tempted me, proved me, and saw my work.

¹⁰Forty years long was I grieved with this generation, and said, It is a people that do err in their heart, and they have not known my ways:

¹¹Unto whom I sware in my wrath that they should not enter into my rest.

# Psalm 96

*God will indeed judge the earth, and those devoted to
His righteousness and truth have nothing to fear.
Nature itself—heavens, seas, fields, and trees—will
celebrate the justice of God.*

¹O sing unto the LORD a new song: sing unto the
LORD, all the earth.
²Sing unto the LORD, bless his name; shew forth
his salvation from day to day.
³Declare his glory among the heathen, his
wonders among all people.
⁴For the LORD is great, and greatly to be praised:
he is to be feared above all gods.
⁵For all the gods of the nations are idols: but the
LORD made the heavens.
⁶Honour and majesty are before him: strength
and beauty are in his sanctuary.
⁷Give unto the LORD, O ye kindreds of the
people, give unto the LORD glory and strength.
⁸Give unto the LORD the glory due unto his
name: bring an offering, and come into his courts.
⁹O worship the LORD in the beauty of holiness:
fear before him, all the earth.
¹⁰Say among the heathen that the LORD reigneth:
the world also shall be established that it shall not
be moved: he shall judge the people righteously.
¹¹Let the heavens rejoice, and let the earth be
glad; let the sea roar, and the fulness thereof.
¹²Let the field be joyful, and all that is therein:
then shall all the trees of the wood rejoice
¹³Before the LORD: for he cometh, for he cometh

to judge the earth: he shall judge the world with righteousness, and the people with his truth.

## PSALM 97

*The psalmist's description of God gives evidence of His unchallenged authority. With a foundation of righteousness and justice, the Lord is surrounded by thick, dark clouds. He is also encircled with fire that destroys those who attempt to oppose Him. His presence is accompanied by lightning that strikes fear in all who see it. All nations witness His glory. Even the mountains and heavens are said to yield to the power and righteousness of God.*

¹The LORD reigneth; let the earth rejoice; let the multitude of isles be glad thereof.
²Clouds and darkness are round about him: righteousness and judgment are the habitation of his throne.
³A fire goeth before him, and burneth up his enemies round about.
⁴His lightnings enlightened the world: the earth saw, and trembled.
⁵The hills melted like wax at the presence of the LORD, at the presence of the Lord of the whole earth.
⁶The heavens declare his righteousness, and all the people see his glory.
⁷Confounded be all they that serve graven images, that boast themselves of idols: worship him, all ye gods.

⁸Zion heard, and was glad; and the daughters of Judah rejoiced because of thy judgments, O LORD.
⁹For thou, LORD, art high above all the earth: thou art exalted far above all gods.
¹⁰Ye that love the LORD, hate evil: he preserveth the souls of his saints; he delivereth them out of the hand of the wicked.
¹¹Light is sown for the righteous, and gladness for the upright in heart.
¹²Rejoice in the LORD, ye righteous; and give thanks at the remembrance of his holiness.

## PSALM 98

*People and nature alike are to respond with joy to the work of God. According to verse 1, He has already done incredible things, but His work is not finished. The whole world can look forward to the day when He will come as judge, bringing righteousness and justice.*

¹O sing unto the LORD a new song; for he hath done marvellous things: his right hand, and his holy arm, hath gotten him the victory.
²The LORD hath made known his salvation: his righteousness hath he openly shewed in the sight of the heathen.
³He hath remembered his mercy and his truth toward the house of Israel: all the ends of the earth have seen the salvation of our God.
⁴Make a joyful noise unto the LORD, all the earth: make a loud noise, and rejoice, and sing praise.
⁵Sing unto the LORD with the harp; with the

harp, and the voice of a psalm.

⁶With trumpets and sound of cornet make a joyful noise before the LORD, the King.

⁷Let the sea roar, and the fulness thereof; the world, and they that dwell therein.

⁸Let the floods clap their hands: let the hills be joyful together

⁹Before the LORD; for he cometh to judge the earth: with righteousness shall he judge the world, and the people with equity.

## PSALM 100

*People have good reason to praise God. To begin with, He is God—the one and only sovereign Lord—a fact to be acknowledged. In addition, He is the Creator. Created humanity should identify with their Creator. Beyond that, God initiated a loving relationship with His people. They are not just created beings left to fend for themselves; they remain in God's care as the sheep of His pasture.*

¹Make a joyful noise unto the LORD, all ye lands.

²Serve the LORD with gladness: come before his presence with singing.

³Know ye that the LORD he is God: it is he that hath made us, and not we ourselves; we are his people, and the sheep of his pasture.

⁴Enter into his gates with thanksgiving, and into his courts with praise: be thankful unto him, and bless his name.

⁵For the LORD is good; his mercy is everlasting; and his truth endureth to all generations.

# Psalm 101

*The Lord is a God of love and justice, and for that
reason David opens his psalm with praise.
But almost immediately, in verse 2, he responds to
the justice of God. He wants to devote himself, both
privately and publicly, to model a blameless life.
And once his heart is blameless, he is determined not to
get involved with things that might corrupt it.*

¹I will sing of mercy and judgment: unto thee, O
LORD, will I sing.
²I will behave myself wisely in a perfect way. O
when wilt thou come unto me? I will walk within
my house with a perfect heart.
³I will set no wicked thing before mine eyes: I
hate the work of them that turn aside; it shall not
cleave to me.
⁴A froward heart shall depart from me: I will not
know a wicked person.
⁵Whoso privily slandereth his neighbour, him will
I cut off: him that hath an high look and a proud
heart will not I suffer.
⁶Mine eyes shall be upon the faithful of the land,
that they may dwell with me: he that walketh in a
perfect way, he shall serve me.
⁷He that worketh deceit shall not dwell within
my house: he that telleth lies shall not tarry in my
sight.
⁸I will early destroy all the wicked of the land;
that I may cut off all wicked doers from the city
of the LORD.

*David realizes that the Lord is a forgiving God. The iniquities of the people had at times resulted in His wrath, but it had been clear that God is slow to become angry and shows mercy to His people. God's wrath tends to get people's attention when nothing else does, but the psalmist points out that God's anger is just as evident as His compassion, grace, and love.*

¹Bless the Lord, O my soul: and all that is within me, bless his holy name.

²Bless the Lord, O my soul, and forget not all his benefits:

³Who forgiveth all thine iniquities; who healeth all thy diseases;

⁴Who redeemeth thy life from destruction; who crowneth thee with lovingkindness and tender mercies;

⁵Who satisfieth thy mouth with good things; so that thy youth is renewed like the eagle's.

⁶The Lord executeth righteousness and judgment for all that are oppressed.

⁷He made known his ways unto Moses, his acts unto the children of Israel.

⁸The Lord is merciful and gracious, slow to anger, and plenteous in mercy.

⁹He will not always chide: neither will he keep his anger for ever.

¹⁰He hath not dealt with us after our sins; nor rewarded us according to our iniquities.

¹¹For as the heaven is high above the earth, so great is his mercy toward them that fear him.

<sup>12</sup>As far as the east is from the west, so far hath he removed our transgressions from us.

<sup>13</sup>Like as a father pitieth his children, so the Lord pitieth them that fear him.

<sup>14</sup>For he knoweth our frame; he remembereth that we are dust.

<sup>15</sup>As for man, his days are as grass: as a flower of the field, so he flourisheth.

<sup>16</sup>For the wind passeth over it, and it is gone; and the place thereof shall know it no more.

<sup>17</sup>But the mercy of the Lord is from everlasting to everlasting upon them that fear him, and his righteousness unto children's children;

<sup>18</sup>To such as keep his covenant, and to those that remember his commandments to do them.

<sup>19</sup>The Lord hath prepared his throne in the heavens; and his kingdom ruleth over all.

<sup>20</sup>Bless the Lord, ye his angels, that excel in strength, that do his commandments, hearkening unto the voice of his word.

<sup>21</sup>Bless ye the Lord, all ye his hosts; ye ministers of his, that do his pleasure.

<sup>22</sup>Bless the Lord, all his works in all places of his dominion: bless the Lord, O my soul.

*God's provision sustains the entire animal kingdom.*
*His presence comforts; His absence terrifies.*
*He supplies life and determines life spans,*
*when it is time to return to the dust.*
*And as impressive as His creation is, God is far greater.*

¹Bless the LORD, O my soul. O LORD my God, thou art very great; thou art clothed with honour and majesty.

²Who coverest thyself with light as with a garment: who stretchest out the heavens like a curtain:

³Who layeth the beams of his chambers in the waters: who maketh the clouds his chariot: who walketh upon the wings of the wind:

⁴Who maketh his angels spirits; his ministers a flaming fire:

⁵Who laid the foundations of the earth, that it should not be removed for ever.

⁶Thou coveredst it with the deep as with a garment: the waters stood above the mountains.

⁷At thy rebuke they fled; at the voice of thy thunder they hasted away.

⁸They go up by the mountains; they go down by the valleys unto the place which thou hast founded for them.

⁹Thou hast set a bound that they may not pass over; that they turn not again to cover the earth.

¹⁰He sendeth the springs into the valleys, which run among the hills.

¹¹They give drink to every beast of the field: the

wild asses quench their thirst.

¹²By them shall the fowls of the heaven have their habitation, which sing among the branches.

¹³He watereth the hills from his chambers: the earth is satisfied with the fruit of thy works.

¹⁴He causeth the grass to grow for the cattle, and herb for the service of man: that he may bring forth food out of the earth;

¹⁵And wine that maketh glad the heart of man, and oil to make his face to shine, and bread which strengtheneth man's heart.

¹⁶The trees of the LORD are full of sap; the cedars of Lebanon, which he hath planted;

¹⁷Where the birds make their nests: as for the stork, the fir trees are her house.

¹⁸The high hills are a refuge for the wild goats; and the rocks for the conies.

¹⁹He appointed the moon for seasons: the sun knoweth his going down.

²⁰Thou makest darkness, and it is night: wherein all the beasts of the forest do creep forth.

²¹The young lions roar after their prey, and seek their meat from God.

²²The sun ariseth, they gather themselves together, and lay them down in their dens.

²³Man goeth forth unto his work and to his labour until the evening.

²⁴O LORD, how manifold are thy works! in wisdom hast thou made them all: the earth is full of thy riches.

²⁵So is this great and wide sea, wherein are things creeping innumerable, both small and great beasts.

²⁶There go the ships: there is that leviathan, whom thou hast made to play therein.

²⁷These wait all upon thee; that thou mayest give them their meat in due season.

²⁸That thou givest them they gather: thou openest thine hand, they are filled with good.

²⁹Thou hidest thy face, they are troubled: thou takest away their breath, they die, and return to their dust.

³⁰Thou sendest forth thy spirit, they are created: and thou renewest the face of the earth.

³¹The glory of the LORD shall endure for ever: the LORD shall rejoice in his works.

³²He looketh on the earth, and it trembleth: he toucheth the hills, and they smoke.

³³I will sing unto the LORD as long as I live: I will sing praise to my God while I have my being.

³⁴My meditation of him shall be sweet: I will be glad in the LORD.

³⁵Let the sinners be consumed out of the earth, and let the wicked be no more. Bless thou the LORD, O my soul. Praise ye the LORD.

*If we think of the psalms as songs,
then Psalm 108 is a medley of Psalms 57 and 60.
Combined as they are here, the psalm is a song of
victory to celebrate God's incomparable love
and faithfulness as displayed in His deliverance
of Israel from their enemies.*

¹O God, my heart is fixed; I will sing and give praise, even with my glory.

²Awake, psaltery and harp: I myself will awake early.

³I will praise thee, O LORD, among the people: and I will sing praises unto thee among the nations.

⁴For thy mercy is great above the heavens: and thy truth reacheth unto the clouds.

⁵Be thou exalted, O God, above the heavens: and thy glory above all the earth;

⁶That thy beloved may be delivered: save with thy right hand, and answer me.

⁷God hath spoken in his holiness; I will rejoice, I will divide Shechem, and mete out the valley of Succoth.

⁸Gilead is mine; Manasseh is mine; Ephraim also is the strength of mine head; Judah is my lawgiver;

⁹Moab is my washpot; over Edom will I cast out my shoe; over Philistia will I triumph.

¹⁰Who will bring me into the strong city? who will lead me into Edom?

¹¹Wilt not thou, O God, who hast cast us off? and

wilt not thou, O God, go forth with our hosts?
¹²Give us help from trouble: for vain is the help of man.
¹³Through God we shall do valiantly: for he it is that shall tread down our enemies.

## PSALM 111

*Popular usage may have diminished the intended definition of the word* awesome. *The meaning here is "awe-inspiring." When someone begins to comprehend the holiness of God, the result is a deep, fearful reverence.*

¹Praise ye the LORD. I will praise the LORD with my whole heart, in the assembly of the upright, and in the congregation.
²The works of the LORD are great, sought out of all them that have pleasure therein.
³His work is honourable and glorious: and his righteousness endureth for ever.
⁴He hath made his wonderful works to be remembered: the LORD is gracious and full of compassion.
⁵He hath given meat unto them that fear him: he will ever be mindful of his covenant.
⁶He hath shewed his people the power of his works, that he may give them the heritage of the heathen.
⁷The works of his hands are verity and judgment; all his commandments are sure.
⁸They stand fast for ever and ever, and are done in truth and uprightness.

⁹He sent redemption unto his people: he hath commanded his covenant for ever: holy and reverend is his name.

¹⁰The fear of the LORD is the beginning of wisdom: a good understanding have all they that do his commandments: his praise endureth for ever.

## PSALM 112

*The psalmist ends this otherwise positive and uplifting psalm with a caveat for those who do not pursue righteousness. Wicked people will witness God's goodness to others and be vexed. Their longings will remain unfulfilled. Rather than praising God, they will grind their teeth and waste away.*

¹Praise ye the LORD. Blessed is the man that feareth the LORD, that delighteth greatly in his commandments.

²His seed shall be mighty upon earth: the generation of the upright shall be blessed.

³Wealth and riches shall be in his house: and his righteousness endureth for ever.

⁴Unto the upright there ariseth light in the darkness: he is gracious, and full of compassion, and righteous.

⁵A good man sheweth favour, and lendeth: he will guide his affairs with discretion.

⁶Surely he shall not be moved for ever: the righteous shall be in everlasting remembrance.

⁷He shall not be afraid of evil tidings: his heart is fixed, trusting in the LORD.

⁸His heart is established, he shall not be afraid, until he see his desire upon his enemies.

⁹He hath dispersed, he hath given to the poor; his righteousness endureth for ever; his horn shall be exalted with honour.

¹⁰The wicked shall see it, and be grieved; he shall gnash with his teeth, and melt away: the desire of the wicked shall perish.

## PSALM 113

*In contrast with the high enthroned and mighty God,*
*all humanity is poor, needy, and barren.*
*So when people begin to comprehend that the great*
*God of the universe has chosen*
*to be actively involved in their lives, they should heed*
*the psalmist's repeated exhortation to praise the Lord.*

¹Praise ye the Lord. Praise, O ye servants of the Lord, praise the name of the Lord.

²Blessed be the name of the Lord from this time forth and for evermore.

³From the rising of the sun unto the going down of the same the Lord's name is to be praised.

⁴The Lord is high above all nations, and his glory above the heavens.

⁵Who is like unto the Lord our God, who dwelleth on high,

⁶Who humbleth himself to behold the things that are in heaven, and in the earth!

⁷He raiseth up the poor out of the dust, and lifteth the needy out of the dunghill;

<sup>8</sup>That he may set him with princes, even with the princes of his people.
<sup>9</sup>He maketh the barren woman to keep house, and to be a joyful mother of children. Praise ye the LORD.

## PSALM 115

*Almost all the surrounding nations worshipped visual, tactile idols that reminded them of their gods. They made them as lifelike as possible. The psalmist's description in verses 5–7 is detailed, with mention of idols with mouths, eyes, ears, noses, hands, feet, and throats. Yet as he makes clear in verse 4, the idols are carved by humans—totally inanimate and impotent.*

<sup>1</sup>Not unto us, O LORD, not unto us, but unto thy name give glory, for thy mercy, and for thy truth's sake.
<sup>2</sup>Wherefore should the heathen say, Where is now their God?
<sup>3</sup>But our God is in the heavens: he hath done whatsoever he hath pleased.
<sup>4</sup>Their idols are silver and gold, the work of men's hands.
<sup>5</sup>They have mouths, but they speak not: eyes have they, but they see not:
<sup>6</sup>They have ears, but they hear not: noses have they, but they smell not:
<sup>7</sup>They have hands, but they handle not: feet have they, but they walk not: neither speak they through their throat.

⁸They that make them are like unto them; so is every one that trusteth in them.

⁹O Israel, trust thou in the Lord: he is their help and their shield.

¹⁰O house of Aaron, trust in the Lord: he is their help and their shield.

¹¹Ye that fear the Lord, trust in the Lord: he is their help and their shield.

¹²The Lord hath been mindful of us: he will bless us; he will bless the house of Israel; he will bless the house of Aaron.

¹³He will bless them that fear the Lord, both small and great.

¹⁴The Lord shall increase you more and more, you and your children.

¹⁵Ye are blessed of the Lord which made heaven and earth.

¹⁶The heaven, even the heavens, are the Lord's: but the earth hath he given to the children of men.

¹⁷The dead praise not the Lord, neither any that go down into silence.

¹⁸But we will bless the Lord from this time forth and for evermore. Praise the Lord.

*Who but God could have changed the psalmist's tears,
stumbling, and nearness to death into a walk in the
land of the living? Apparently everyone else had
lacked the faith that God would deliver him, creating
great dismay. But the psalmist had believed,
and God had restored him to health and safety.*

¹I love the LORD, because he hath heard my voice and my supplications.

²Because he hath inclined his ear unto me, therefore will I call upon him as long as I live.

³The sorrows of death compassed me, and the pains of hell gat hold upon me: I found trouble and sorrow.

⁴Then called I upon the name of the LORD; O LORD, I beseech thee, deliver my soul.

⁵Gracious is the LORD, and righteous; yea, our God is merciful.

⁶The LORD preserveth the simple: I was brought low, and he helped me.

⁷Return unto thy rest, O my soul; for the LORD hath dealt bountifully with thee.

⁸For thou hast delivered my soul from death, mine eyes from tears, and my feet from falling.

⁹I will walk before the LORD in the land of the living.

¹⁰I believed, therefore have I spoken: I was greatly afflicted:

¹¹I said in my haste, All men are liars.

¹²What shall I render unto the LORD for all his benefits toward me?

¹³I will take the cup of salvation, and call upon the name of the LORD.

¹⁴I will pay my vows unto the LORD now in the presence of all his people.

¹⁵Precious in the sight of the LORD is the death of his saints.

¹⁶O LORD, truly I am thy servant; I am thy servant, and the son of thine handmaid: thou hast loosed my bonds.

¹⁷I will offer to thee the sacrifice of thanksgiving, and will call upon the name of the LORD.

¹⁸I will pay my vows unto the LORD now in the presence of all his people,

¹⁹In the courts of the LORD's house, in the midst of thee, O Jerusalem. Praise ye the LORD.

## PSALM 121

*The protection of God is the theme of Psalm 121. Pilgrimages could be dangerous journeys with both geographical challenges and criminal elements to contend with. As the psalmist looks upward toward Jerusalem, his destination, he acknowledges that his help comes from God, who had created those mountains.*

¹I will lift up mine eyes unto the hills, from whence cometh my help.

²My help cometh from the LORD, which made heaven and earth.

³He will not suffer thy foot to be moved: he that keepeth thee will not slumber.

⁴Behold, he that keepeth Israel shall neither

slumber nor sleep.

⁵The LORD is thy keeper: the LORD is thy shade upon thy right hand.

⁶The sun shall not smite thee by day, nor the moon by night.

⁷The LORD shall preserve thee from all evil: he shall preserve thy soul.

⁸The LORD shall preserve thy going out and thy coming in from this time forth, and even for evermore.

## PSALM 122

*Jerusalem means "city of peace," an appropriate title in the days of David and Solomon. But those people who sang this psalm in the period following the exile of Israel would soon realize how turbulent the recent history of Jerusalem had been. The call to pray for the peace of Jerusalem probably has more significance in later years.*

¹I was glad when they said unto me, Let us go into the house of the LORD.

²Our feet shall stand within thy gates, O Jerusalem.

³Jerusalem is builded as a city that is compact together:

⁴Whither the tribes go up, the tribes of the LORD, unto the testimony of Israel, to give thanks unto the name of the LORD.

⁵For there are set thrones of judgment, the thrones of the house of David.

⁶Pray for the peace of Jerusalem: they shall prosper that love thee.

⁷Peace be within thy walls, and prosperity within thy palaces.
⁸For my brethren and companions' sakes, I will now say, Peace be within thee.
⁹Because of the house of the LORD our God I will seek thy good.

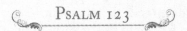

## PSALM 123

*It is not uncommon for those who are devoted to God to suffer ridicule or contempt from those who are not believers. In such cases, it is difficult to ignore the verbal jeers, yet the psalmist has been able to divert his attention and place his eyes on the Lord. With no thought of personal revenge or frontier justice, he leaves the matter in God's hands.*

¹Unto thee lift I up mine eyes, O thou that dwellest in the heavens.
²Behold, as the eyes of servants look unto the hand of their masters, and as the eyes of a maiden unto the hand of her mistress; so our eyes wait upon the LORD our God, until that he have mercy upon us.
³Have mercy upon us, O LORD, have mercy upon us: for we are exceedingly filled with contempt.
⁴Our soul is exceedingly filled with the scorning of those that are at ease, and with the contempt of the proud.

# Psalm 127

*Whether the topic is domestic life, national security,
or family trees, God should be acknowledged
as the source of all success and contentment.*

¹Except the LORD build the house, they labour in
vain that build it: except the LORD keep the city,
the watchman waketh but in vain.
²It is vain for you to rise up early, to sit up late,
to eat the bread of sorrows: for so he giveth his
beloved sleep.
³Lo, children are an heritage of the LORD: and the
fruit of the womb is his reward.
⁴As arrows are in the hand of a mighty man; so
are children of the youth.
⁵Happy is the man that hath his quiver full of
them: they shall not be ashamed, but they shall
speak with the enemies in the gate.

*The psalmist realizes that God is not a heavenly recorder
of wrongs—no one would ever be able to please Him.
God chose to forgive the sins of His people, which is an
astounding fact. The response, then, should be reverential
fear of God—not cowering in panic or horror but
willfully submitting to Him in worship and obedience.*

¹Out of the depths have I cried unto thee, O
LORD.
²Lord, hear my voice: let thine ears be attentive to
the voice of my supplications.
³If thou, LORD, shouldest mark iniquities, O Lord,
who shall stand?
⁴But there is forgiveness with thee, that thou
mayest be feared.
⁵I wait for the LORD, my soul doth wait, and in
his word do I hope.
⁶My soul waiteth for the Lord more than they
that watch for the morning: I say, more than they
that watch for the morning.
⁷Let Israel hope in the LORD: for with the
LORD there is mercy, and with him is plenteous
redemption.
⁸And he shall redeem Israel from all his iniquities.

*Verses 6–7 are reminders that God's power is seen in all
of nature—earth, skies, and seas. Clouds, wind, rain,
and lightning are all part of His wonderful design.
But God is not limited to working through nature. He
is a God of miracles that defy the laws of nature.
In verses 8–9, the psalmist recalls the plagues sent upon
Egypt—perhaps the best known of God's miracles.*

¹Praise ye the LORD. Praise ye the name of the
LORD; praise him, O ye servants of the LORD.
²Ye that stand in the house of the LORD, in the
courts of the house of our God,
³Praise the LORD; for the LORD is good: sing
praises unto his name; for it is pleasant.
⁴For the LORD hath chosen Jacob unto himself,
and Israel for his peculiar treasure.
⁵For I know that the LORD is great, and that our
Lord is above all gods.
⁶Whatsoever the LORD pleased, that did he in
heaven, and in earth, in the seas, and all deep
places.
⁷He causeth the vapours to ascend from the ends
of the earth; he maketh lightnings for the rain; he
bringeth the wind out of his treasuries.
⁸Who smote the firstborn of Egypt, both of man
and beast.
⁹Who sent tokens and wonders into the midst of
thee, O Egypt, upon Pharaoh, and upon all his
servants.
¹⁰Who smote great nations, and slew mighty
kings;

¹¹Sihon king of the Amorites, and Og king of Bashan, and all the kingdoms of Canaan:

¹²And gave their land for an heritage, an heritage unto Israel his people.

¹³Thy name, O LORD, endureth for ever; and thy memorial, O LORD, throughout all generations.

¹⁴For the LORD will judge his people, and he will repent himself concerning his servants.

¹⁵The idols of the heathen are silver and gold, the work of men's hands.

¹⁶They have mouths, but they speak not; eyes have they, but they see not;

¹⁷They have ears, but they hear not; neither is there any breath in their mouths.

¹⁸They that make them are like unto them: so is every one that trusteth in them.

¹⁹Bless the LORD, O house of Israel: bless the LORD, O house of Aaron:

²⁰Bless the LORD, O house of Levi: ye that fear the LORD, bless the LORD.

²¹Blessed be the LORD out of Zion, which dwelleth at Jerusalem. Praise ye the LORD.

*There are many reasons to give thanks to God.*
*But at the top of the list, as the psalmist reminds his*
*listeners twenty-six times during this song,*
*God should be thanked because His love endures forever.*

¹O give thanks unto the LORD; for he is good: for his mercy endureth for ever.

²O give thanks unto the God of gods: for his mercy endureth for ever.

³O give thanks to the Lord of lords: for his mercy endureth for ever.

⁴To him who alone doeth great wonders: for his mercy endureth for ever.

⁵To him that by wisdom made the heavens: for his mercy endureth for ever.

⁶To him that stretched out the earth above the waters: for his mercy endureth for ever.

⁷To him that made great lights: for his mercy endureth for ever:

⁸The sun to rule by day: for his mercy endureth for ever:

⁹The moon and stars to rule by night: for his mercy endureth for ever.

¹⁰To him that smote Egypt in their firstborn: for his mercy endureth for ever:

¹¹And brought out Israel from among them: for his mercy endureth for ever:

¹²With a strong hand, and with a stretched out arm: for his mercy endureth for ever.

¹³To him which divided the Red sea into parts: for his mercy endureth for ever:

[14]And made Israel to pass through the midst of it: for his mercy endureth for ever:

[15]But overthrew Pharaoh and his host in the Red sea: for his mercy endureth for ever.

[16]To him which led his people through the wilderness: for his mercy endureth for ever.

[17]To him which smote great kings: for his mercy endureth for ever:

[18]And slew famous kings: for his mercy endureth for ever:

[19]Sihon king of the Amorites: for his mercy endureth for ever:

[20]And Og the king of Bashan: for his mercy endureth for ever:

[21]And gave their land for an heritage: for his mercy endureth for ever:

[22]Even an heritage unto Israel his servant: for his mercy endureth for ever.

[23]Who remembered us in our low estate: for his mercy endureth for ever:

[24]And hath redeemed us from our enemies: for his mercy endureth for ever.

[25]Who giveth food to all flesh: for his mercy endureth for ever.

[26]O give thanks unto the God of heaven: for his mercy endureth for ever.

# Psalm 138

*God is highly exalted, yet He is always
willing to respond to the lowly—
those who humble themselves and seek His help.
Those who attempt to exalt themselves in pride, however,
miss out on God's compassionate help and support.*

¹I will praise thee with my whole heart: before the gods will I sing praise unto thee.
²I will worship toward thy holy temple, and praise thy name for thy lovingkindness and for thy truth: for thou hast magnified thy word above all thy name.
³In the day when I cried thou answeredst me, and strengthenedst me with strength in my soul.
⁴All the kings of the earth shall praise thee, O LORD, when they hear the words of thy mouth.
⁵Yea, they shall sing in the ways of the LORD: for great is the glory of the LORD.
⁶Though the LORD be high, yet hath he respect unto the lowly: but the proud he knoweth afar off.
⁷Though I walk in the midst of trouble, thou wilt revive me: thou shalt stretch forth thine hand against the wrath of mine enemies, and thy right hand shall save me.
⁸The LORD will perfect that which concerneth me: thy mercy, O LORD, endureth for ever: forsake not the works of thine own hands.

*Verses 23–24 offer one of the most fascinating challenges of scripture. David had certainly committed some grievous sins against God on occasion. But at this point in his life, he is able to ask God to examine both his actions and his thoughts to attempt to detect anything offensive or improper. Few people get to a point in their spiritual lives where they will consider making such an invitation.*

¹O Lord, thou hast searched me, and known me.
²Thou knowest my downsitting and mine uprising, thou understandest my thought afar off.
³Thou compassest my path and my lying down, and art acquainted with all my ways.
⁴For there is not a word in my tongue, but, lo, O Lord, thou knowest it altogether.
⁵Thou hast beset me behind and before, and laid thine hand upon me.
⁶Such knowledge is too wonderful for me; it is high, I cannot attain unto it.
⁷Whither shall I go from thy spirit? or whither shall I flee from thy presence?
⁸If I ascend up into heaven, thou art there: if I make my bed in hell, behold, thou art there.
⁹If I take the wings of the morning, and dwell in the uttermost parts of the sea;
¹⁰Even there shall thy hand lead me, and thy right hand shall hold me.
¹¹If I say, Surely the darkness shall cover me; even the night shall be light about me.
¹²Yea, the darkness hideth not from thee; but the

night shineth as the day: the darkness and the light are both alike to thee.

¹³For thou hast possessed my reins: thou hast covered me in my mother's womb.

¹⁴I will praise thee; for I am fearfully and wonderfully made: marvellous are thy works; and that my soul knoweth right well.

¹⁵My substance was not hid from thee, when I was made in secret, and curiously wrought in the lowest parts of the earth.

¹⁶Thine eyes did see my substance, yet being unperfect; and in thy book all my members were written, which in continuance were fashioned, when as yet there was none of them.

¹⁷How precious also are thy thoughts unto me, O God! how great is the sum of them!

¹⁸If I should count them, they are more in number than the sand: when I awake, I am still with thee.

¹⁹Surely thou wilt slay the wicked, O God: depart from me therefore, ye bloody men.

²⁰For they speak against thee wickedly, and thine enemies take thy name in vain.

²¹Do not I hate them, O LORD, that hate thee? and am not I grieved with those that rise up against thee?

²²I hate them with perfect hatred: I count them mine enemies.

²³Search me, O God, and know my heart: try me, and know my thoughts:

²⁴And see if there be any wicked way in me, and lead me in the way everlasting.

*People in need will especially be glad for the gifts of God. He is loving, He honors His promises, He uplifts the fallen, He provides food, and He is the source that can satisfy all desires. For all these reasons and more, David concludes this psalm with his final expression of praise to God, inviting every living thing to join him.*

¹I will extol thee, my God, O king; and I will bless thy name for ever and ever.
²Every day will I bless thee; and I will praise thy name for ever and ever.
³Great is the LORD, and greatly to be praised; and his greatness is unsearchable.
⁴One generation shall praise thy works to another, and shall declare thy mighty acts.
⁵I will speak of the glorious honour of thy majesty, and of thy wondrous works.
⁶And men shall speak of the might of thy terrible acts: and I will declare thy greatness.
⁷They shall abundantly utter the memory of thy great goodness, and shall sing of thy righteousness.
⁸The LORD is gracious, and full of compassion; slow to anger, and of great mercy.
⁹The LORD is good to all: and his tender mercies are over all his works.
¹⁰All thy works shall praise thee, O LORD; and thy saints shall bless thee.
¹¹They shall speak of the glory of thy kingdom, and talk of thy power;
¹²To make known to the sons of men his mighty

acts, and the glorious majesty of his kingdom.

¹³Thy kingdom is an everlasting kingdom, and thy dominion endureth throughout all generations.

¹⁴The LORD upholdeth all that fall, and raiseth up all those that be bowed down.

¹⁵The eyes of all wait upon thee; and thou givest them their meat in due season.

¹⁶Thou openest thine hand, and satisfiest the desire of every living thing.

¹⁷The LORD is righteous in all his ways, and holy in all his works.

¹⁸The LORD is nigh unto all them that call upon him, to all that call upon him in truth.

¹⁹He will fulfil the desire of them that fear him: he also will hear their cry, and will save them.

²⁰The LORD preserveth all them that love him: but all the wicked will he destroy.

²¹My mouth shall speak the praise of the LORD: and let all flesh bless his holy name for ever and ever.

*When people need help, they have a choice.*
*They can depend on other people or they can turn*
*to God. This psalm offers praise to God*
*because He is always dependable.*

¹Praise ye the LORD. Praise the LORD, O my soul.
²While I live will I praise the LORD: I will sing
praises unto my God while I have any being.
³Put not your trust in princes, nor in the son of
man, in whom there is no help.
⁴His breath goeth forth, he returneth to his earth;
in that very day his thoughts perish.
⁵Happy is he that hath the God of Jacob for his
help, whose hope is in the LORD his God:
⁶Which made heaven, and earth, the sea, and all
that therein is: which keepeth truth for ever:
⁷Which executeth judgment for the oppressed:
which giveth food to the hungry. The LORD
looseth the prisoners:
⁸The LORD openeth the eyes of the blind: the
LORD raiseth them that are bowed down: the
LORD loveth the righteous:
⁹The LORD preserveth the strangers; he relieveth
the fatherless and widow: but the way of the
wicked he turneth upside down.
¹⁰The LORD shall reign for ever, even thy God, O
Zion, unto all generations. Praise ye the LORD.

*The psalmist reminds everyone that the same God who
helped them is the One who had created, numbered,
and named the stars. His understanding and His
power are unlimited. And while His power
will be used to subdue the wicked,
it will always provide support for the humble.*

¹Praise ye the LORD: for it is good to sing praises
unto our God; for it is pleasant; and praise is
comely.

²The LORD doth build up Jerusalem: he gathereth
together the outcasts of Israel.

³He healeth the broken in heart, and bindeth up
their wounds.

⁴He telleth the number of the stars; he calleth
them all by their names.

⁵Great is our Lord, and of great power: his
understanding is infinite.

⁶The LORD lifteth up the meek: he casteth the
wicked down to the ground.

⁷Sing unto the LORD with thanksgiving; sing
praise upon the harp unto our God:

⁸Who covereth the heaven with clouds, who
prepareth rain for the earth, who maketh grass to
grow upon the mountains.

⁹He giveth to the beast his food, and to the young
ravens which cry.

¹⁰He delighteth not in the strength of the horse:
he taketh not pleasure in the legs of a man.

¹¹The LORD taketh pleasure in them that fear him,
in those that hope in his mercy.

¹²Praise the LORD, O Jerusalem; praise thy God, O Zion.

¹³For he hath strengthened the bars of thy gates; he hath blessed thy children within thee.

¹⁴He maketh peace in thy borders, and filleth thee with the finest of the wheat.

¹⁵He sendeth forth his commandment upon earth: his word runneth very swiftly.

¹⁶He giveth snow like wool: he scattereth the hoarfrost like ashes.

¹⁷He casteth forth his ice like morsels: who can stand before his cold?

¹⁸He sendeth out his word, and melteth them: he causeth his wind to blow, and the waters flow.

¹⁹He sheweth his word unto Jacob, his statutes and his judgments unto Israel.

²⁰He hath not dealt so with any nation: and as for his judgments, they have not known them. Praise ye the LORD.

*The horn mentioned in verse 14 is a symbol for power
that frequently represents the king.
But sometimes, and this may be one such case, the
horn is symbolic of the glory God has provided for His
people. God's people are close to His heart, and for that
reason (among many others) He should be praised.*

¹Praise ye the LORD. Praise ye the LORD from the heavens: praise him in the heights.

²Praise ye him, all his angels: praise ye him, all his hosts.

³Praise ye him, sun and moon: praise him, all ye stars of light.

⁴Praise him, ye heavens of heavens, and ye waters that be above the heavens.

⁵Let them praise the name of the LORD: for he commanded, and they were created.

⁶He hath also stablished them for ever and ever: he hath made a decree which shall not pass.

⁷Praise the LORD from the earth, ye dragons, and all deeps:

⁸Fire, and hail; snow, and vapours; stormy wind fulfilling his word:

⁹Mountains, and all hills; fruitful trees, and all cedars:

¹⁰Beasts, and all cattle; creeping things, and flying fowl:

¹¹Kings of the earth, and all people; princes, and all judges of the earth:

¹²Both young men, and maidens; old men, and children:

<sup>13</sup>Let them praise the name of the LORD: for his name alone is excellent; his glory is above the earth and heaven.

<sup>14</sup>He also exalteth the horn of his people, the praise of all his saints; even of the children of Israel, a people near unto him. Praise ye the LORD.

## PSALM 149

*The people should praise God for their salvation. According to verses 2–5, their praise should take various enthusiastic forms, including dancing, tambourine and harp music*

<sup>1</sup>Praise ye the LORD. Sing unto the LORD a new song, and his praise in the congregation of saints.

<sup>2</sup>Let Israel rejoice in him that made him: let the children of Zion be joyful in their King.

<sup>3</sup>Let them praise his name in the dance: let them sing praises unto him with the timbrel and harp.

<sup>4</sup>For the LORD taketh pleasure in his people: he will beautify the meek with salvation.

<sup>5</sup>Let the saints be joyful in glory: let them sing aloud upon their beds.

<sup>6</sup>Let the high praises of God be in their mouth, and a two-edged sword in their hand;

<sup>7</sup>To execute vengeance upon the heathen, and punishments upon the people;

<sup>8</sup>To bind their kings with chains, and their nobles with fetters of iron;

<sup>9</sup>To execute upon them the judgment written: this honour have all his saints. Praise ye the LORD.

# PSALM 150

*Psalm 1 appears to be positioned intentionally to introduce the book of Psalms. Similarly, this concluding psalm may have been written to close the book with a final emphasis on the importance of praise. The psalm (and the book of Psalms) concludes with one final "Praise the Lord."*

¹Praise ye the LORD. Praise God in his sanctuary: praise him in the firmament of his power.
²Praise him for his mighty acts: praise him according to his excellent greatness.
³Praise him with the sound of the trumpet: praise him with the psaltery and harp.
⁴Praise him with the timbrel and dance: praise him with stringed instruments and organs.
⁵Praise him upon the loud cymbals: praise him upon the high sounding cymbals.
⁶Let every thing that hath breath praise the LORD. Praise ye the LORD.

*The Hebrew word translated* knowledge *in verse 7 is a synonym for* wisdom. *This type of knowledge is not just possessing information; it is the ability to apply that information in real life.*

[1]The proverbs of Solomon the son of David, king of Israel;

[2]To know wisdom and instruction; to perceive the words of understanding;

[3]To receive the instruction of wisdom, justice, and judgment, and equity;

[4]To give subtilty to the simple, to the young man knowledge and discretion.

[5]A wise man will hear, and will increase learning; and a man of understanding shall attain unto wise counsels:

[6]To understand a proverb, and the interpretation; the words of the wise, and their dark sayings.

[7]The fear of the LORD is the beginning of knowledge: but fools despise wisdom and instruction.

[8]My son, hear the instruction of thy father, and forsake not the law of thy mother:

[9]For they shall be an ornament of grace unto thy head, and chains about thy neck.

[10]My son, if sinners entice thee, consent thou not.

[11]If they say, Come with us, let us lay wait for blood, let us lurk privily for the innocent without cause:

[12]Let us swallow them up alive as the grave; and whole, as those that go down into the pit:

[13]We shall find all precious substance, we shall fill

our houses with spoil:

¹⁴Cast in thy lot among us; let us all have one purse:

¹⁵My son, walk not thou in the way with them; refrain thy foot from their path:

¹⁶For their feet run to evil, and make haste to shed blood.

¹⁷Surely in vain the net is spread in the sight of any bird.

¹⁸And they lay wait for their own blood; they lurk privily for their own lives.

¹⁹So are the ways of every one that is greedy of gain; which taketh away the life of the owners thereof.

²⁰Wisdom crieth without; she uttereth her voice in the streets:

²¹She crieth in the chief place of concourse, in the openings of the gates: in the city she uttereth her words, saying,

²²How long, ye simple ones, will ye love simplicity? and the scorners delight in their scorning, and fools hate knowledge?

²³Turn you at my reproof: behold, I will pour out my spirit unto you, I will make known my words unto you.

²⁴Because I have called, and ye refused; I have stretched out my hand, and no man regarded;

²⁵But ye have set at nought all my counsel, and would none of my reproof:

²⁶I also will laugh at your calamity; I will mock when your fear cometh;

²⁷When your fear cometh as desolation, and your

destruction cometh as a whirlwind; when distress and anguish cometh upon you.

<sup>28</sup>Then shall they call upon me, but I will not answer; they shall seek me early, but they shall not find me:

<sup>29</sup>For that they hated knowledge, and did not choose the fear of the LORD:

<sup>30</sup>They would none of my counsel: they despised all my reproof.

<sup>31</sup>Therefore shall they eat of the fruit of their own way, and be filled with their own devices.

<sup>32</sup>For the turning away of the simple shall slay them, and the prosperity of fools shall destroy them.

<sup>33</sup>But whoso hearkeneth unto me shall dwell safely, and shall be quiet from fear of evil.

*If a person seeks wisdom from God, many things will happen. He will understand what is right—how the holiness of God is meant to express itself in time and space. He will be a person who is fair, good, and noble. He will know what path to take and what decisions to make.*

¹My son, if thou wilt receive my words, and hide my commandments with thee;

²So that thou incline thine ear unto wisdom, and apply thine heart to understanding;

³Yea, if thou criest after knowledge, and liftest up thy voice for understanding;

⁴If thou seekest her as silver, and searchest for her as for hid treasures;

⁵Then shalt thou understand the fear of the LORD, and find the knowledge of God.

⁶For the LORD giveth wisdom: out of his mouth cometh knowledge and understanding.

⁷He layeth up sound wisdom for the righteous: he is a buckler to them that walk uprightly.

⁸He keepeth the paths of judgment, and preserveth the way of his saints.

⁹Then shalt thou understand righteousness, and judgment, and equity; yea, every good path.

¹⁰When wisdom entereth into thine heart, and knowledge is pleasant unto thy soul;

¹¹Discretion shall preserve thee, understanding shall keep thee:

¹²To deliver thee from the way of the evil man, from the man that speaketh froward things;

¹³Who leave the paths of uprightness, to walk in the ways of darkness;

¹⁴Who rejoice to do evil, and delight in the frowardness of the wicked;

¹⁵Whose ways are crooked, and they froward in their paths:

¹⁶To deliver thee from the strange woman, even from the stranger which flattereth with her words;

¹⁷Which forsaketh the guide of her youth, and forgetteth the covenant of her God.

¹⁸For her house inclineth unto death, and her paths unto the dead.

¹⁹None that go unto her return again, neither take they hold of the paths of life.

²⁰That thou mayest walk in the way of good men, and keep the paths of the righteous.

²¹For the upright shall dwell in the land, and the perfect shall remain in it.

²²But the wicked shall be cut off from the earth, and the transgressors shall be rooted out of it.

*What one has around the neck—close to the throat—*
*influences one's words, and words reflect character.*
*The heart refers to the core of what motivates all that*
*one does. Thus, the whole person is to be influenced*
*by love and faithfulness.*

[1]My son, forget not my law; but let thine heart keep my commandments:

[2]For length of days, and long life, and peace, shall they add to thee.

[3]Let not mercy and truth forsake thee: bind them about thy neck; write them upon the table of thine heart:

[4]So shalt thou find favour and good understanding in the sight of God and man.

[5]Trust in the LORD with all thine heart; and lean not unto thine own understanding.

[6]In all thy ways acknowledge him, and he shall direct thy paths.

[7]Be not wise in thine own eyes: fear the LORD, and depart from evil.

[8]It shall be health to thy navel, and marrow to thy bones.

[9]Honour the LORD with thy substance, and with the firstfruits of all thine increase:

[10]So shall thy barns be filled with plenty, and thy presses shall burst out with new wine.

[11]My son, despise not the chastening of the LORD; neither be weary of his correction:

[12]For whom the LORD loveth he correcteth; even as a father the son in whom he delighteth.

¹³Happy is the man that findeth wisdom, and the man that getteth understanding.

¹⁴For the merchandise of it is better than the merchandise of silver, and the gain thereof than fine gold.

¹⁵She is more precious than rubies: and all the things thou canst desire are not to be compared unto her.

¹⁶Length of days is in her right hand; and in her left hand riches and honour.

¹⁷Her ways are ways of pleasantness, and all her paths are peace.

¹⁸She is a tree of life to them that lay hold upon her: and happy is every one that retaineth her.

¹⁹The LORD by wisdom hath founded the earth; by understanding hath he established the heavens.

²⁰By his knowledge the depths are broken up, and the clouds drop down the dew.

²¹My son, let not them depart from thine eyes: keep sound wisdom and discretion:

²²So shall they be life unto thy soul, and grace to thy neck.

²³Then shalt thou walk in thy way safely, and thy foot shall not stumble.

²⁴When thou liest down, thou shalt not be afraid: yea, thou shalt lie down, and thy sleep shall be sweet.

²⁵Be not afraid of sudden fear, neither of the desolation of the wicked, when it cometh.

²⁶For the LORD shall be thy confidence, and shall keep thy foot from being taken.

²⁷Withhold not good from them to whom it is

due, when it is in the power of thine hand to do it.

²⁸Say not unto thy neighbour, Go, and come again, and to morrow I will give; when thou hast it by thee.

²⁹Devise not evil against thy neighbour, seeing he dwelleth securely by thee.

³⁰Strive not with a man without cause, if he have done thee no harm.

³¹Envy thou not the oppressor, and choose none of his ways.

³²For the froward is abomination to the LORD: but his secret is with the righteous.

³³The curse of the LORD is in the house of the wicked: but he blesseth the habitation of the just.

³⁴Surely he scorneth the scorners: but he giveth grace unto the lowly.

³⁵The wise shall inherit glory: but shame shall be the promotion of fools.

*The warning to move neither to the right nor to the left is also found in Deuteronomy 5:32, 17:11, 28:14 and Joshua 23:6. The idea is that one should not be distracted from the way of wisdom. The way of wisdom should not be ignored, added to, or subtracted from. Wisdom provides the way of life, and everything around it is the way of destruction.*

¹Hear, ye children, the instruction of a father, and attend to know understanding.

²For I give you good doctrine, forsake ye not my law.

³For I was my father's son, tender and only beloved in the sight of my mother.

⁴He taught me also, and said unto me, Let thine heart retain my words: keep my commandments, and live.

⁵Get wisdom, get understanding: forget it not; neither decline from the words of my mouth.

⁶Forsake her not, and she shall preserve thee: love her, and she shall keep thee.

⁷Wisdom is the principal thing; therefore get wisdom: and with all thy getting get understanding.

⁸Exalt her, and she shall promote thee: she shall bring thee to honour, when thou dost embrace her.

⁹She shall give to thine head an ornament of grace: a crown of glory shall she deliver to thee.

¹⁰Hear, O my son, and receive my sayings; and the years of thy life shall be many.

¹¹I have taught thee in the way of wisdom; I have led thee in right paths.

¹²When thou goest, thy steps shall not be straitened; and when thou runnest, thou shalt not stumble.
¹³Take fast hold of instruction; let her not go: keep her; for she is thy life.
¹⁴Enter not into the path of the wicked, and go not in the way of evil men.
¹⁵Avoid it, pass not by it, turn from it, and pass away.
¹⁶For they sleep not, except they have done mischief; and their sleep is taken away, unless they cause some to fall.
¹⁷For they eat the bread of wickedness, and drink the wine of violence.
¹⁸But the path of the just is as the shining light, that shineth more and more unto the perfect day.
¹⁹The way of the wicked is as darkness: they know not at what they stumble.
²⁰My son, attend to my words; incline thine ear unto my sayings.
²¹Let them not depart from thine eyes; keep them in the midst of thine heart.
²²For they are life unto those that find them, and health to all their flesh.
²³Keep thy heart with all diligence; for out of it are the issues of life.
²⁴Put away from thee a froward mouth, and perverse lips put far from thee.
²⁵Let thine eyes look right on, and let thine eyelids look straight before thee.
²⁶Ponder the path of thy feet, and let all thy ways be established.
²⁷Turn not to the right hand nor to the left: remove thy foot from evil.

*God has not made His wisdom inaccessible; His wisdom is available to all those who seek it. When wisdom arrives, she will bestow blessings and treasures on those who love and seek her. But improper motives with the pursuit of wisdom do not mix. In other words, we cannot try to pursue wisdom for the sake of gain. Rather, the pursuit of wisdom is the pursuit of the things that God loves for the purpose of the glory of God.*

¹Doth not wisdom cry? and understanding put forth her voice?

²She standeth in the top of high places, by the way in the places of the paths.

³She crieth at the gates, at the entry of the city, at the coming in at the doors.

⁴Unto you, O men, I call; and my voice is to the sons of man.

⁵O ye simple, understand wisdom: and, ye fools, be ye of an understanding heart.

⁶Hear; for I will speak of excellent things; and the opening of my lips shall be right things.

⁷For my mouth shall speak truth; and wickedness is an abomination to my lips.

⁸All the words of my mouth are in righteousness; there is nothing froward or perverse in them.

⁹They are all plain to him that understandeth, and right to them that find knowledge.

¹⁰Receive my instruction, and not silver; and knowledge rather than choice gold.

¹¹For wisdom is better than rubies; and all the things that may be desired are not to be compared to it.

¹²I wisdom dwell with prudence, and find out knowledge of witty inventions.

¹³The fear of the LORD is to hate evil: pride, and arrogancy, and the evil way, and the froward mouth, do I hate.

¹⁴Counsel is mine, and sound wisdom: I am understanding; I have strength.

¹⁵By me kings reign, and princes decree justice.

¹⁶By me princes rule, and nobles, even all the judges of the earth.

¹⁷I love them that love me; and those that seek me early shall find me.

¹⁸Riches and honour are with me; yea, durable riches and righteousness.

¹⁹My fruit is better than gold, yea, than fine gold; and my revenue than choice silver.

²⁰I lead in the way of righteousness, in the midst of the paths of judgment:

²¹That I may cause those that love me to inherit substance; and I will fill their treasures.

²²The LORD possessed me in the beginning of his way, before his works of old.

²³I was set up from everlasting, from the beginning, or ever the earth was.

²⁴When there were no depths, I was brought forth; when there were no fountains abounding with water.

²⁵Before the mountains were settled, before the hills was I brought forth:

²⁶While as yet he had not made the earth, nor the fields, nor the highest part of the dust of the world.

<sup>27</sup>When he prepared the heavens, I was there: when he set a compass upon the face of the depth:

<sup>28</sup>When he established the clouds above: when he strengthened the fountains of the deep:

<sup>29</sup>When he gave to the sea his decree, that the waters should not pass his commandment: when he appointed the foundations of the earth:

<sup>30</sup>Then I was by him, as one brought up with him: and I was daily his delight, rejoicing always before him;

<sup>31</sup>Rejoicing in the habitable part of his earth; and my delights were with the sons of men.

<sup>32</sup>Now therefore hearken unto me, O ye children: for blessed are they that keep my ways.

<sup>33</sup>Hear instruction, and be wise, and refuse it not.

<sup>34</sup>Blessed is the man that heareth me, watching daily at my gates, waiting at the posts of my doors.

<sup>35</sup>For whoso findeth me findeth life, and shall obtain favour of the LORD.

<sup>36</sup>But he that sinneth against me wrongeth his own soul: all they that hate me love death.

*The simple point of the passage is that if we
enter wisdom's house, we will have life.
Yet this point is made in some complex ways.
The nature of wisdom's house of
seven pillars is uncertain.*

¹Wisdom hath builded her house, she hath hewn
out her seven pillars:

²She hath killed her beasts; she hath mingled her
wine; she hath also furnished her table.

³She hath sent forth her maidens: she crieth upon
the highest places of the city,

⁴Whoso is simple, let him turn in hither: as for
him that wanteth understanding, she saith to him,

⁵Come, eat of my bread, and drink of the wine
which I have mingled.

⁶Forsake the foolish, and live; and go in the way
of understanding.

⁷He that reproveth a scorner getteth to himself
shame: and he that rebuketh a wicked man
getteth himself a blot.

⁸Reprove not a scorner, lest he hate thee: rebuke a
wise man, and he will love thee.

⁹Give instruction to a wise man, and he will be
yet wiser: teach a just man, and he will increase in
learning.

¹⁰The fear of the LORD is the beginning of
wisdom: and the knowledge of the holy is
understanding.

¹¹For by me thy days shall be multiplied, and the
years of thy life shall be increased.

¹²If thou be wise, thou shalt be wise for thyself: but if thou scornest, thou alone shalt bear it.

¹³A foolish woman is clamorous: she is simple, and knoweth nothing.

¹⁴For she sitteth at the door of her house, on a seat in the high places of the city,

¹⁵To call passengers who go right on their ways:

¹⁶Whoso is simple, let him turn in hither: and as for him that wanteth understanding, she saith to him,

¹⁷Stolen waters are sweet, and bread eaten in secret is pleasant.

¹⁸But he knoweth not that the dead are there; and that her guests are in the depths of hell.

# PROVERBS 10

*The contrast between a righteous person and a wicked person is common in Proverbs. Solomon wants his son to understand this difference, so here he sets out to explain it.*

¹The proverbs of Solomon. A wise son maketh a glad father: but a foolish son is the heaviness of his mother.

²Treasures of wickedness profit nothing: but righteousness delivereth from death.

³The LORD will not suffer the soul of the righteous to famish: but he casteth away the substance of the wicked.

⁴He becometh poor that dealeth with a slack hand: but the hand of the diligent maketh rich.

<sup>5</sup>He that gathereth in summer is a wise son: but he that sleepeth in harvest is a son that causeth shame.

<sup>6</sup>Blessings are upon the head of the just: but violence covereth the mouth of the wicked.

<sup>7</sup>The memory of the just is blessed: but the name of the wicked shall rot.

<sup>8</sup>The wise in heart will receive commandments: but a prating fool shall fall.

<sup>9</sup>He that walketh uprightly walketh surely: but he that perverteth his ways shall be known.

<sup>10</sup>He that winketh with the eye causeth sorrow: but a prating fool shall fall.

<sup>11</sup>The mouth of a righteous man is a well of life: but violence covereth the mouth of the wicked.

<sup>12</sup>Hatred stirreth up strifes: but love covereth all sins.

<sup>13</sup>In the lips of him that hath understanding wisdom is found: but a rod is for the back of him that is void of understanding.

<sup>14</sup>Wise men lay up knowledge: but the mouth of the foolish is near destruction.

<sup>15</sup>The rich man's wealth is his strong city: the destruction of the poor is their poverty.

<sup>16</sup>The labour of the righteous tendeth to life: the fruit of the wicked to sin.

<sup>17</sup>He is in the way of life that keepeth instruction: but he that refuseth reproof erreth.

<sup>18</sup>He that hideth hatred with lying lips, and he that uttereth a slander, is a fool.

<sup>19</sup>In the multitude of words there wanteth not sin: but he that refraineth his lips is wise.

<sup>20</sup>The tongue of the just is as choice silver: the heart of the wicked is little worth.

<sup>21</sup>The lips of the righteous feed many: but fools die for want of wisdom.

<sup>22</sup>The blessing of the LORD, it maketh rich, and he addeth no sorrow with it.

<sup>23</sup>It is as sport to a fool to do mischief: but a man of understanding hath wisdom.

<sup>24</sup>The fear of the wicked, it shall come upon him: but the desire of the righteous shall be granted.

<sup>25</sup>As the whirlwind passeth, so is the wicked no more: but the righteous is an everlasting foundation.

<sup>26</sup>As vinegar to the teeth, and as smoke to the eyes, so is the sluggard to them that send him.

<sup>27</sup>The fear of the LORD prolongeth days: but the years of the wicked shall be shortened.

<sup>28</sup>The hope of the righteous shall be gladness: but the expectation of the wicked shall perish.

<sup>29</sup>The way of the LORD is strength to the upright: but destruction shall be to the workers of iniquity.

<sup>30</sup>The righteous shall never be removed: but the wicked shall not inhabit the earth.

<sup>31</sup>The mouth of the just bringeth forth wisdom: but the froward tongue shall be cut out.

<sup>32</sup>The lips of the righteous know what is acceptable: but the mouth of the wicked speaketh frowardness.

*To receive the tree of life is to have an abundant life that cannot be taken away. To gain that abundant life, one must practice obedience, learn from people worthy of respect, and not act rashly.*

¹A wise son heareth his father's instruction: but a scorner heareth not rebuke.

²A man shall eat good by the fruit of his mouth: but the soul of the transgressors shall eat violence.

³He that keepeth his mouth keepeth his life: but he that openeth wide his lips shall have destruction.

⁴The soul of the sluggard desireth, and hath nothing: but the soul of the diligent shall be made fat.

⁵A righteous man hateth lying: but a wicked man is loathsome, and cometh to shame.

⁶Righteousness keepeth him that is upright in the way: but wickedness overthroweth the sinner.

⁷There is that maketh himself rich, yet hath nothing: there is that maketh himself poor, yet hath great riches.

⁸The ransom of a man's life are his riches: but the poor heareth not rebuke.

⁹The light of the righteous rejoiceth: but the lamp of the wicked shall be put out.

¹⁰Only by pride cometh contention: but with the well advised is wisdom.

¹¹Wealth gotten by vanity shall be diminished: but he that gathereth by labour shall increase.

¹²Hope deferred maketh the heart sick: but when

the desire cometh, it is a tree of life.

¹³Whoso despiseth the word shall be destroyed: but he that feareth the commandment shall be rewarded.

¹⁴The law of the wise is a fountain of life, to depart from the snares of death.

¹⁵Good understanding giveth favour: but the way of transgressors is hard.

¹⁶Every prudent man dealeth with knowledge: but a fool layeth open his folly.

¹⁷A wicked messenger falleth into mischief: but a faithful ambassador is health.

¹⁸Poverty and shame shall be to him that refuseth instruction: but he that regardeth reproof shall be honoured.

¹⁹The desire accomplished is sweet to the soul: but it is abomination to fools to depart from evil.

²⁰He that walketh with wise men shall be wise: but a companion of fools shall be destroyed.

²¹Evil pursueth sinners: but to the righteous good shall be repayed.

²²A good man leaveth an inheritance to his children's children: and the wealth of the sinner is laid up for the just.

²³Much food is in the tillage of the poor: but there is that is destroyed for want of judgment.

²⁴He that spareth his rod hateth his son: but he that loveth him chasteneth him betimes.

²⁵The righteous eateth to the satisfying of his soul: but the belly of the wicked shall want.

*A person cannot control his experience with this world
from the outside in; it has to be from the inside out.
A wise person seeks to understand the world from
God's point of view, which brings joy to the heart.
A happy heart has a continual feast. In fact, to have a
heart feasting on the joy, fear, and love of the Lord
is better than a literal feast.*

¹A soft answer turneth away wrath: but grievous words stir up anger.

²The tongue of the wise useth knowledge aright: but the mouth of fools poureth out foolishness.

³The eyes of the LORD are in every place, beholding the evil and the good.

⁴A wholesome tongue is a tree of life: but perverseness therein is a breach in the spirit.

⁵A fool despiseth his father's instruction: but he that regardeth reproof is prudent.

⁶In the house of the righteous is much treasure: but in the revenues of the wicked is trouble.

⁷The lips of the wise disperse knowledge: but the heart of the foolish doeth not so.

⁸The sacrifice of the wicked is an abomination to the LORD: but the prayer of the upright is his delight.

⁹The way of the wicked is an abomination unto the LORD: but he loveth him that followeth after righteousness.

¹⁰Correction is grievous unto him that forsaketh the way: and he that hateth reproof shall die.

¹¹Hell and destruction are before the LORD: how

much more then the hearts of the children of men?

<sup>12</sup>A scorner loveth not one that reproveth him: neither will he go unto the wise.

<sup>13</sup>A merry heart maketh a cheerful countenance: but by sorrow of the heart the spirit is broken.

<sup>14</sup>The heart of him that hath understanding seeketh knowledge: but the mouth of fools feedeth on foolishness.

<sup>15</sup>All the days of the afflicted are evil: but he that is of a merry heart hath a continual feast.

<sup>16</sup>Better is little with the fear of the LORD than great treasure and trouble therewith.

<sup>17</sup>Better is a dinner of herbs where love is, than a stalled ox and hatred therewith.

<sup>18</sup>A wrathful man stirreth up strife: but he that is slow to anger appeaseth strife.

<sup>19</sup>The way of the slothful man is as an hedge of thorns: but the way of the righteous is made plain.

<sup>20</sup>A wise son maketh a glad father: but a foolish man despiseth his mother.

<sup>21</sup>Folly is joy to him that is destitute of wisdom: but a man of understanding walketh uprightly.

<sup>22</sup>Without counsel purposes are disappointed: but in the multitude of counsellors they are established.

<sup>23</sup>A man hath joy by the answer of his mouth: and a word spoken in due season, how good is it!

<sup>24</sup>The way of life is above to the wise, that he may depart from hell beneath.

<sup>25</sup>The LORD will destroy the house of the proud: but he will establish the border of the widow.

<sup>26</sup>The thoughts of the wicked are an abomination

to the LORD: but the words of the pure are pleasant words.

<sup>27</sup>He that is greedy of gain troubleth his own house; but he that hateth gifts shall live.

<sup>28</sup>The heart of the righteous studieth to answer: but the mouth of the wicked poureth out evil things.

<sup>29</sup>The LORD is far from the wicked: but he heareth the prayer of the righteous.

<sup>30</sup>The light of the eyes rejoiceth the heart: and a good report maketh the bones fat.

<sup>31</sup>The ear that heareth the reproof of life abideth among the wise.

<sup>32</sup>He that refuseth instruction despiseth his own soul: but he that heareth reproof getteth understanding.

<sup>33</sup>The fear of the LORD is the instruction of wisdom; and before honour is humility.

*Verse 33 concludes the chapter as it had begun,
with a reminder that the sovereignty of God directs all
human activity. People have a number of ways to decide
how to proceed in life, but they should be thankful that
God is the One whose will is ultimately accomplished.*

¹The preparations of the heart in man, and the
answer of the tongue, is from the LORD.

²All the ways of a man are clean in his own eyes;
but the LORD weigheth the spirits.

³Commit thy works unto the LORD, and thy
thoughts shall be established.

⁴The LORD hath made all things for himself: yea,
even the wicked for the day of evil.

⁵Every one that is proud in heart is an
abomination to the LORD: though hand join in
hand, he shall not be unpunished.

⁶By mercy and truth iniquity is purged: and by the
fear of the LORD men depart from evil.

⁷When a man's ways please the LORD, he maketh
even his enemies to be at peace with him.

⁸Better is a little with righteousness than great
revenues without right.

⁹A man's heart deviseth his way: but the LORD
directeth his steps.

¹⁰A divine sentence is in the lips of the king: his
mouth transgresseth not in judgment.

¹¹A just weight and balance are the LORD's: all the
weights of the bag are his work.

¹²It is an abomination to kings to commit wickedness: for the throne is established by righteousness.

¹³Righteous lips are the delight of kings; and they love him that speaketh right.

¹⁴The wrath of a king is as messengers of death: but a wise man will pacify it.

¹⁵In the light of the king's countenance is life; and his favour is as a cloud of the latter rain.

¹⁶How much better is it to get wisdom than gold! and to get understanding rather to be chosen than silver!

¹⁷The highway of the upright is to depart from evil: he that keepeth his way preserveth his soul.

¹⁸Pride goeth before destruction, and an haughty spirit before a fall.

¹⁹Better it is to be of an humble spirit with the lowly, than to divide the spoil with the proud.

²⁰He that handleth a matter wisely shall find good: and whoso trusteth in the Lord, happy is he.

²¹The wise in heart shall be called prudent: and the sweetness of the lips increaseth learning.

²²Understanding is a wellspring of life unto him that hath it: but the instruction of fools is folly.

²³The heart of the wise teacheth his mouth, and addeth learning to his lips.

²⁴Pleasant words are as an honeycomb, sweet to the soul, and health to the bones.

²⁵There is a way that seemeth right unto a man, but the end thereof are the ways of death.

²⁶He that laboureth laboureth for himself; for his mouth craveth it of him.

²⁷An ungodly man diggeth up evil: and in his lips there is as a burning fire.

²⁸A froward man soweth strife: and a whisperer separateth chief friends.

<sup>29</sup>A violent man enticeth his neighbour, and leadeth him into the way that is not good.
<sup>30</sup>He shutteth his eyes to devise froward things: moving his lips he bringeth evil to pass.
<sup>31</sup>The hoary head is a crown of glory, if it be found in the way of righteousness.
<sup>32</sup>He that is slow to anger is better than the mighty; and he that ruleth his spirit than he that taketh a city.
<sup>33</sup>The lot is cast into the lap; but the whole disposing thereof is of the LORD.

## PROVERBS 18

*While words can be misused in any number of ways, when used properly they can edify others. Verse 20 suggests that just as food satisfies one's hunger, well-chosen words can be an equally pleasurable source of contentment. Wise people take their words seriously.*

<sup>1</sup>Through desire a man, having separated himself, seeketh and intermeddleth with all wisdom.
<sup>2</sup>A fool hath no delight in understanding, but that his heart may discover itself.
<sup>3</sup>When the wicked cometh, then cometh also contempt, and with ignominy reproach.
<sup>4</sup>The words of a man's mouth are as deep waters, and the wellspring of wisdom as a flowing brook.
<sup>5</sup>It is not good to accept the person of the wicked, to overthrow the righteous in judgment.
<sup>6</sup>A fool's lips enter into contention, and his mouth calleth for strokes.

⁷A fool's mouth is his destruction, and his lips are the snare of his soul.

⁸The words of a talebearer are as wounds, and they go down into the innermost parts of the belly.

⁹He also that is slothful in his work is brother to him that is a great waster.

¹⁰The name of the LORD is a strong tower: the righteous runneth into it, and is safe.

¹¹The rich man's wealth is his strong city, and as an high wall in his own conceit.

¹²Before destruction the heart of man is haughty, and before honour is humility.

¹³He that answereth a matter before he heareth it, it is folly and shame unto him.

¹⁴The spirit of a man will sustain his infirmity; but a wounded spirit who can bear?

¹⁵The heart of the prudent getteth knowledge; and the ear of the wise seeketh knowledge.

¹⁶A man's gift maketh room for him, and bringeth him before great men.

¹⁷He that is first in his own cause seemeth just; but his neighbour cometh and searcheth him.

¹⁸The lot causeth contentions to cease, and parteth between the mighty.

¹⁹A brother offended is harder to be won than a strong city: and their contentions are like the bars of a castle.

²⁰A man's belly shall be satisfied with the fruit of his mouth; and with the increase of his lips shall he be filled.

²¹Death and life are in the power of the tongue: and they that love it shall eat the fruit thereof.

<sup>22</sup>Whoso findeth a wife findeth a good thing, and obtaineth favour of the LORD.
<sup>23</sup>The poor useth intreaties; but the rich answereth roughly.
<sup>24</sup>A man that hath friends must shew himself friendly: and there is a friend that sticketh closer than a brother.

## PROVERBS 22

*Verse 6 is probably one of the most quoted from the book of Proverbs. Like many others, this proverb is true in a general (not an absolute) sense. When parents fear God, seek wisdom, get their priorities straight, and attempt to instill the same things in their children, those children have a much better likelihood of learning to make good decisions on their own.*

<sup>1</sup>A good name is rather to be chosen than great riches, and loving favour rather than silver and gold.
<sup>2</sup>The rich and poor meet together: the LORD is the maker of them all.
<sup>3</sup>A prudent man foreseeth the evil, and hideth himself: but the simple pass on, and are punished.
<sup>4</sup>By humility and the fear of the LORD are riches, and honour, and life.
<sup>5</sup>Thorns and snares are in the way of the froward: he that doth keep his soul shall be far from them.
<sup>6</sup>Train up a child in the way he should go: and when he is old, he will not depart from it.
<sup>7</sup>The rich ruleth over the poor, and the borrower is servant to the lender.

⁸He that soweth iniquity shall reap vanity: and the rod of his anger shall fail.

⁹He that hath a bountiful eye shall be blessed; for he giveth of his bread to the poor.

¹⁰Cast out the scorner, and contention shall go out; yea, strife and reproach shall cease.

¹¹He that loveth pureness of heart, for the grace of his lips the king shall be his friend.

¹²The eyes of the LORD preserve knowledge, and he overthroweth the words of the transgressor.

¹³The slothful man saith, There is a lion without, I shall be slain in the streets.

¹⁴The mouth of strange women is a deep pit: he that is abhorred of the LORD shall fall therein.

¹⁵Foolishness is bound in the heart of a child; but the rod of correction shall drive it far from him.

¹⁶He that oppresseth the poor to increase his riches, and he that giveth to the rich, shall surely come to want.

¹⁷Bow down thine ear, and hear the words of the wise, and apply thine heart unto my knowledge.

¹⁸For it is a pleasant thing if thou keep them within thee; they shall withal be fitted in thy lips.

¹⁹That thy trust may be in the LORD, I have made known to thee this day, even to thee.

²⁰Have not I written to thee excellent things in counsels and knowledge,

²¹That I might make thee know the certainty of the words of truth; that thou mightest answer the words of truth to them that send unto thee?

²²Rob not the poor, because he is poor: neither oppress the afflicted in the gate:

²³For the LORD will plead their cause, and spoil the soul of those that spoiled them.

²⁴Make no friendship with an angry man; and with a furious man thou shalt not go:

²⁵Lest thou learn his ways, and get a snare to thy soul.

²⁶Be not thou one of them that strike hands, or of them that are sureties for debts.

²⁷If thou hast nothing to pay, why should he take away thy bed from under thee?

²⁸Remove not the ancient landmark, which thy fathers have set.

²⁹Seest thou a man diligent in his business? he shall stand before kings; he shall not stand before mean men.

*Just as a house is constructed and then filled with goods that make it livable, a commitment to wisdom builds up people, and ongoing knowledge edifies them and allows them to function together.*

¹Be not thou envious against evil men, neither desire to be with them.

²For their heart studieth destruction, and their lips talk of mischief.

³Through wisdom is an house builded; and by understanding it is established:

⁴And by knowledge shall the chambers be filled with all precious and pleasant riches.

⁵A wise man is strong; yea, a man of knowledge increaseth strength.

⁶For by wise counsel thou shalt make thy war: and in multitude of counsellors there is safety.

⁷Wisdom is too high for a fool: he openeth not his mouth in the gate.

⁸He that deviseth to do evil shall be called a mischievous person.

⁹The thought of foolishness is sin: and the scorner is an abomination to men.

¹⁰If thou faint in the day of adversity, thy strength is small.

¹¹If thou forbear to deliver them that are drawn unto death, and those that are ready to be slain;

¹²If thou sayest, Behold, we knew it not; doth not he that pondereth the heart consider it? and he that keepeth thy soul, doth not he know it? and shall not he render to every man according to his works?

¹³My son, eat thou honey, because it is good; and the honeycomb, which is sweet to thy taste:

¹⁴So shall the knowledge of wisdom be unto thy soul: when thou hast found it, then there shall be a reward, and thy expectation shall not be cut off.

¹⁵Lay not wait, O wicked man, against the dwelling of the righteous; spoil not his resting place:

¹⁶For a just man falleth seven times, and riseth up again: but the wicked shall fall into mischief.

¹⁷Rejoice not when thine enemy falleth, and let not thine heart be glad when he stumbleth:

¹⁸Lest the LORD see it, and it displease him, and he turn away his wrath from him.

¹⁹Fret not thyself because of evil men, neither be thou envious at the wicked;

²⁰For there shall be no reward to the evil man; the candle of the wicked shall be put out.

²¹My son, fear thou the LORD and the king: and meddle not with them that are given to change:

²²For their calamity shall rise suddenly; and who knoweth the ruin of them both?

²³These things also belong to the wise. It is not good to have respect of persons in judgment.

²⁴He that saith unto the wicked, Thou are righteous; him shall the people curse, nations shall abhor him:

²⁵But to them that rebuke him shall be delight, and a good blessing shall come upon them.

²⁶Every man shall kiss his lips that giveth a right answer.

²⁷Prepare thy work without, and make it fit for thyself in the field; and afterwards build thine house.

[28]Be not a witness against thy neighbour without cause; and deceive not with thy lips.

[29]Say not, I will do so to him as he hath done to me: I will render to the man according to his work.

[30]I went by the field of the slothful, and by the vineyard of the man void of understanding;

[31]And, lo, it was all grown over with thorns, and nettles had covered the face thereof, and the stone wall thereof was broken down.

[32]Then I saw, and considered it well: I looked upon it, and received instruction.

[33]Yet a little sleep, a little slumber, a little folding of the hands to sleep:

[34]So shall thy poverty come as one that travelleth; and thy want as an armed man.

*A real friend is willing to tell the truth and say the tough things. When tough things have to be said, it is more dangerous to leave and ignore those tough words than to stay and endure them. Through friendship people are challenged, changed, refreshed, and supported.*

¹Boast not thyself of to morrow; for thou knowest not what a day may bring forth.

²Let another man praise thee, and not thine own mouth; a stranger, and not thine own lips.

³A stone is heavy, and the sand weighty; but a fool's wrath is heavier than them both.

⁴Wrath is cruel, and anger is outrageous; but who is able to stand before envy?

⁵Open rebuke is better than secret love.

⁶Faithful are the wounds of a friend; but the kisses of an enemy are deceitful.

⁷The full soul loatheth an honeycomb; but to the hungry soul every bitter thing is sweet.

⁸As a bird that wandereth from her nest, so is a man that wandereth from his place.

⁹Ointment and perfume rejoice the heart: so doth the sweetness of a man's friend by hearty counsel.

¹⁰Thine own friend, and thy father's friend, forsake not; neither go into thy brother's house in the day of thy calamity: for better is a neighbour that is near than a brother far off.

¹¹My son, be wise, and make my heart glad, that I may answer him that reproacheth me.

¹²A prudent man foreseeth the evil, and hideth

himself; but the simple pass on, and are punished.

¹³Take his garment that is surety for a stranger, and take a pledge of him for a strange woman.

¹⁴He that blesseth his friend with a loud voice, rising early in the morning, it shall be counted a curse to him.

¹⁵A continual dropping in a very rainy day and a contentious woman are alike.

¹⁶Whosoever hideth her hideth the wind, and the ointment of his right hand, which bewrayeth itself.

¹⁷Iron sharpeneth iron; so a man sharpeneth the countenance of his friend.

¹⁸Whoso keepeth the fig tree shall eat the fruit thereof: so he that waiteth on his master shall be honoured.

¹⁹As in water face answereth to face, so the heart of man to man.

²⁰Hell and destruction are never full; so the eyes of man are never satisfied.

²¹As the fining pot for silver, and the furnace for gold; so is a man to his praise.

²²Though thou shouldest bray a fool in a mortar among wheat with a pestle, yet will not his foolishness depart from him.

²³Be thou diligent to know the state of thy flocks, and look well to thy herds.

²⁴For riches are not for ever: and doth the crown endure to every generation?

²⁵The hay appeareth, and the tender grass sheweth itself, and herbs of the mountains are gathered.

²⁶The lambs are for thy clothing, and the goats are